E

Loose!
On Letting Stuff Go

Illustrated by Mariyana Nikolova
Edited by Ayesha Ehsan

ISBN: 9798351290751
Printed by Amazon Kindle Direct Publishing

Second print, July 2023

www.einzelganger.co

Thank you supporters and subscribers.

– Einzelgänger

Contents

Introduction

When my uncle passed away in 2011, his funeral card showed the following quote: "True love is letting go" (*Echte liefde is loslaten*). I've pondered over that little sentence for years. My initial interpretation was that true love meant the ability to let go of the deceased, as in my uncle. But how is losing someone to death love? How can it be truer than the love we experience towards the living? It just didn't make sense to me. Later, when I became familiar with Eastern philosophies during my university studies, the connection between love and letting go became clearer to me.

To me, love always had a possessive element to it. Love also included a certain conditionality. Loving someone created expectations. And when these expectations weren't met, I'd be sad and angry. But above all, loving someone implied attachment. In fact, how I experienced love *was* attachment (and to an extent, still is). Hence, loving was often passionate but painful, ecstatic but apprehensive. Especially romantic love, which, when I look back at it, was a matter of despair and emotional instability rather than enjoyment. Passionate romance nevertheless remains sought after by many as an ultimate concern – a supreme goal to attain, even when it involves so much pain; a pain that I had experienced several times through breakups and unrequited love. Or put more lucidly: through losing or not-attaining what I intensely desired. Luckily, further philosophical inquiry led me to radically change my views about love. I finally began to comprehend the relationship between love and letting go. Furthermore, the painful consequences of attachments, in general, became more apparent; the destructive qualities of strong desires and aversions, the importance we attach to the opinions of others, our worries about the future, and ruminations about the past.

Letting go became a focus during my further development. It started with the realization that I was hopelessly attached. All those fetters that I had been creating for myself had been causing tremendous amounts of hurt. Anxiety, depression, and anger were my default state. The teachings of Epictetus, a Stoic philosopher from ancient Greece, have been playing a major role in the process of loosening my unhealthy attachments to the outside world – admittingly, I'm not a Stoic sage, but there has been an improvement. Epictetus pointed out that if we tie ourselves to external circumstances, these very circumstances control us as puppet masters. When fate gives us what we want, we're elated. When it gives us what we don't want, we're in distress. But when the strings are loose, or even absent, then the fickle outside world hardly moves us. And the less we're moved by circumstances, the less power the puppet masters have, and the more tranquil we are in the face of destiny.

Why true love is letting go? Because it's permitting the world to be free. By letting go we make peace with fate; we're okay with people having different opinions, the uncertainty of the future, the dreadfulness of the past, and the impermanence of everything. If we hold on to the world, we try to bend it to our will and seek to control it, which is impossible and not very loving. But if we let go of the world, we accept it as it is; even if that means we lose the world. And yes, we may indeed lose the world, but in return, we gain the gift of being content without it. I'm not sure if my relatives had this elaboration of 'letting go' in mind when they created my uncle's funeral cards, but it's a personal interpretation that makes sense to me and fits the theme of this selection of writings.

This book isn't for ascetics or people who search to attain enlightenment of some sort. It doesn't promote any specific spiritual path or a fortunate afterlife, nor does it promise complete detachment from the outside world. There isn't a specific goal. However, it might encourage the reader to reflect on the many worldly things we needlessly cling to. How do these attachments take shape? What are the consequences? And what can we do about them? The collected works found in *Loose* reflect the open-mindedness of the Einzelgänger YouTube channel, as there are many different perspectives, ideas, and topics to explore: from rejecting the bondage of perfectionism to exploring the benefits of celibacy, letting go of an ex-lover, and appreciating simplicity over the accumulation of material objects.

As with the previous book, *Stoicism for Inner Peace*, you're about to read a collection of essays that I originally published in video format, but decided to bundle into a book after a careful revision. *Stoicism for Inner Peace* was a pretty concise collection of short works on Stoic philosophy. In comparison, this book is a bit scattered, as it contains the influences from many schools of thought, and explores subjects that aren't necessarily connected: from sex to minimalism. However, the underlying theme of not grasping, not holding on, acceptance, and letting go binds these texts together. As a whole, it's a countermovement – or even better: a rebellion – against a society obsessed with accomplishment and prestige, that celebrates toxic passionate love and unhealthy attachment, and favors greed over contentment. Hopefully, the following ruminations inspire the reader to unfasten the reins a little bit.

Kind regards,

Einzelgänger

Letting Go of Other People's Opinions

Rejection

Living in absolute poverty, the great cynic philosopher Diogenes slept in public places and begged for food. One day, he begged in front of a statue. When someone asked him why he did so, Diogenes answered: "to get practice in being refused." For a beggar, being denied food is part of his existence. And even though this experience can be painful, he'll starve if he doesn't face it. But if he trains himself to become indifferent towards it, he'll have no problem asking people for food and might even get it.

Similarly, many people fear being rejected because they experience it as painful. As a result, they avoid situations in which they could be rejected. And so, they rather not apply for jobs that might be out of their league, avoid asking out a romantic interest when there's a possibility of refusal (which is always the case), and never ask friends to hang out as they might turn down the offer. But when we fear rejection, what do we fear? Is it the disapproval from other people? And if so, why do we care so much about that? Or could it be that we fear the idea of being inadequate?

When we look at our species, we see that human beings love to be part of something. Often, we wish to belong to the people around us; we want to be in relationships, and we long to be part of something bigger than ourselves. However, to achieve this, we generally need approval from other people.

11

Who rejects us?

Other people determine whether or not we're good enough to be part of the group. We experience this phenomenon in the playground when we're small children when the other children have to assess if we're good enough to join a game of "hide and seek". Later, the popular kids decide who sits at their table during lunch break. And, when we're adults, other people decide if we're qualified for specific jobs, the right fit for certain social groups and settings, and even if we're eligible for a romantic relationship. If we want something in life that requires other people's approval, we'll eventually face rejection.

In many cases, rejection is based on logic and reason. For example, rejection is an expected and reasonable outcome if someone in a wheelchair applies for being a professional soccer player. Or when someone without any relevant education, work experience, or skills wishes to become the CEO of Google, rejection is inevitable. In such cases, we're simply not skilled enough for the task. In many other situations, rejection doesn't always seem fair. People may reject us for flimsy reasons, like clothing style, even though we'd be highly compatible in other areas. Despite sharing many interests, potential friends may dislike us because of our looks. A nightclub may deny us entrance for the same reasons, even though we could have become long-term customers.

A company may choose another candidate based on physical features rather than skills and experience.

Despite the superficiality and irrationality of people's judgments, those who face rejections often feel personally humiliated. Being rejected by those we're romantically interested in leads to feelings of inadequacy. When people reject us, we believe we're not good enough. The more rejections, the stronger this idea becomes. But, according to Arthur Schopenhauer, we make a mistake if we take too seriously the judgments of other people:

> *"(Apart from this,) what goes on in other people's consciousness is, as such, a matter of indifference to us; and in time we get really indifferent to it, when we come to see how superficial and futile are most people's thoughts, how narrow their ideas, how mean their sentiments, how perverse their opinions, and how much of error there is in most of them; when we learn by experience with what depreciation a man will speak of his fellow when he is not obliged to fear him, or thinks that what he says will not come to his ears. And if ever we have had an opportunity of seeing how the greatest of men will meet with nothing but slight from half-a-dozen blockheads, we shall understand that to lay great value upon what other people say is to pay them too much honor."*

Arthur Schopenhauer, *The Wisdom of Life*, chapter 4

Rejection isn't just about us; it's also about those rejecting us. Rejection isn't always based on facts, reason, and logic but often on people's opinions and feelings. People's opinions are often irrational or plain stupid. So, if someone rejects us, we may want to remind ourselves of Schopenhauer's words.

Amor fati

If we look at rejection from a Stoic point of view, we'll discover that the pain of rejection originates from a wrong attitude towards the world. Rejection means that we don't get what we desire, which is the acceptance and approval of others. So, when we fear rejection, we fear not getting a specific outcome. For example, a man approaches a woman in a bar because he desires to be with her. But if he approaches her and clarifies his intentions, there's a risk of rejection, meaning that the woman isn't romantically or sexually interested in the man. If that happens, the man doesn't achieve the desired outcome.

Stoic philosopher Epictetus explained that we should be careful with desire and aversion. If we don't get what we desire, we feel disappointed, and if we encounter what we're averse to, we experience distress. Hence, he advises us not to desire things to happen as we wish but as they happen. Doing so neutralizes the pain that usually

14

follows after rejection because we don't dread rejection but welcome it: we wish for things to happen as they happen.

Moreover, we could say that rejection is impossible if we don't want to get something out of the situation in the first place. Suppose we simply approach someone just to approach without any expectation or desire for more. There's no rejection if that person doesn't want to talk to us because we've already achieved what we wanted to do, namely, the approach itself. Anything more, whether it would be a friendly conversation, an exchange of phone numbers, or a sexual encounter, is an added extra, which the Stoics classify as a 'preferred indifferent.' According to the Stoics, a preferred indifferent is nice to have but unnecessary to be happy, and it's not in our control and therefore unreliable. So, the result of the approach lies in the hands of fate.

The Stoic idea of Amor Fati means that we embrace fate and thus do not attach ourselves to specific outcomes. How can we feel rejected if we're okay with whatever happens? Suppose we, instead, let our happiness and joy depend on the desired result, like obtaining a romantic relationship with a specific person. In that case, our happiness and contentment depend on that person's actions. As Epictetus stated:

"If someone put you in chains and put you in the custody of some random passerby, you would be

angry. But if you give control of your mind to any
random person who curses you, leaving you
flustered, shouldn't you be ashamed of that?"

Epictetus, *Enchiridion*, 28

If we experience pain through what we perceive as rejection, then we have given control over our minds to another person. But if we just focus on our *own* actions, and embrace any outcome, then the reactions of others don't hurt us, and what we previously saw as rejection will be nothing more than an insignificant movement of fate.

The power of uselessness

Isn't there an advantage to every disadvantage? Doesn't every cloud have a silver lining? Seeing the positive in the negative is a recurring theme in Taoist texts. How can we approach the hardships of life intelligently and make the best out of situations that would generally be seen as undesirable?

The Taoist book Zhuangzi contains a story about a large, crooked tree that every logger refused to chop down. The reason was that loggers looked for straight trees that were fit to create planks. But the crooked tree was so deformed that no carpenter would be able to use it, and so it was left alone, as opposed to its straight brothers and sisters, that were chopped by the boatload. Zhuangzi said to Huizi, the owner of the crooked tree:

> *"You, Sir, have a large tree and are troubled because it is of no use - why do you not plant it in a tract where there is nothing else, or in a wide and barren wild? There you might saunter idly by its side, or in the enjoyment of untroubled ease sleep beneath it. Neither bill nor ax would shorten its existence; there would be nothing to injure it. What is there in its uselessness to cause you distress?"*

Zhuangzi, *Inner Chapters*, Enjoyment in Untroubled Ease (paragraph 7)

The loggers rejected the large, crooked tree, as they saw it as useless. But, as a consequence, it was able to grow old, and some people even considered it sacred. Hence, rejection of any sort doesn't have to be wrong; it may actually be a blessing in disguise. For example, a girl rejects a boy solely based on his clothing style, even though he has a lot in common with her in terms of personality. On the one hand, the boy is disappointed because the girl he likes isn't romantically interested in him. On the other hand, the rejection saved him from being with a shallow person, which could have led to more disappointment and other forms of suffering in the future. Or let's say someone not so smart or talented is

17

mostly passed over and thus misses most opportunities that more intelligent, capable, and talented people get. We could see this as unfortunate. On the other hand, people leave this person alone, and his shoulders don't carry the heavy burdens that those highly esteemed individuals bear due to their many responsibilities. His life is generally more tranquil. And so, rejection can be a good thing if one sees and appreciates not having to suffer the things one would have otherwise encountered.

The straight trees from Zhuangzi's story may have been eligible (and thus not rejected by woodcutters); the sole fact that they were suitable for human use meant that they were chopped down and turned into planks. The woodcutter's refusal to chop down the crooked tree caused its longevity. Being useless in the eyes of others could be great for one's health, as it deprives one of the stress and sacrifice of being useful. Moreover, rejection may signal that we're probably designed for different purposes and that our talents lie elsewhere. For example, the crooked tree wasn't suitable for making wooden planks but later on attracted people because of its uniqueness and old age. So, we may not be meant to work in a specific field, have children, be part of the popular people at school, or be the captain of the soccer team. And, as a consequence of being denied from partaking in all these things, we found a different, more suitable, and unique path.

The Need for Approval

A very curious characteristic of human beings is their desire for being liked. In the early days of mankind, acceptance by the tribe was necessary to stay alive. But in the current age, aside from abiding by the law, we don't need people's validation in order to survive. Sure, the approval of other people is enjoyable and can be a pathway towards opportunities on a personal as well as a professional level. However, spending our energy on seeking approval also comes with a price.

If there's anything that holds us back from being authentic, it's when we design our lives with the purpose of appeasing others. We can do this in many ways, shapes, and forms. But the more we *value* opinions, the less we value our *own* inherent worth. Regardless of what our consumerist society wants us to believe: self-worth is ultimately an indicator of how we appreciate ourselves, regardless of other people's opinions. If we decide that our worth depends on how others perceive us, then this is what we sign up for. Our sense of well-being becomes dependent on what other people think, and because this is not up to us, it's a slavish way to live. In the end, we aren't the ones who decide what our "slave masters" think about us. And when they don't like us anymore despite our efforts, our self-worth is destroyed.

By seeking validation, we lead lives that are *not* our own. When we are sensitive to peer pressure, we may engage in activities that we don't really like. This could be listening to a certain music genre, using substances, or supporting certain political or religious views, just so as to gain approval and acceptance. Sure, by doing this we become part of the herd, but we aren't being very authentic, are we? Because we hide who we truly are. Aren't we deceiving ourselves this way? And, aren't we lying to our environment?

Paradoxically, a person that lives authentically, and doesn't seek other people's approval, gains more respect than someone whose only goal is to appease. This is because people are often attracted to those that are unapologetically themselves, and, ironically, these individuals usually don't care too much about the fact that people are so attracted to them. What clings, repels. What moves freely, attracts. We can say 'no' when everyone says 'yes;' not because we want to be special or rebellious, but simply because we stay true to ourselves. We can allow ourselves to feel hurt, without the need to prove the validity of our suffering to other people. We can walk away and mean it because we know we have to walk away from them to be whole.

When we stop seeking approval, we make our true colors come to the surface. The approval that comes at us naturally, simply for what we manifest by being who we are, is directed at us, and not at this mask that makes our true selves invisible. Isn't it much better to be appreciated by *one* person because of who we wish to be than to be loved by thousands because we fit their requirements? As Jim Carrey once said and I quote:

> *"Your need for acceptance can make you invisible in this world. Don't let anything stand in the way of the light that shines through this form."*

Herd Mentality

Oh, how we are concerned with that animalistic tendency of wanting to belong to the herd. We're not very different from sheep, are we? And mostly, if we don't belong, we feel pretty miserable as we're doomed to the realm of outcasts. You might have experienced the dreadfulness of not belonging in your youth, when you weren't invited to a party, or couldn't sit with the cool kids during lunch. Or maybe you're just the odd one out in your family, or the town's fool. Whatever the case may be, many regards not belonging as painful. Not being part of the herd can evoke loneliness, bitterness, resentment, and even flat-out rage. We just have to look at certain incidents by so-called 'lone wolves' to conclude that the experience of alienation can be harmful to some. However, history also provides many examples of those that went against the grain, lived outside the norm, let go of the herd, and thrived. For the majority, not belonging is a punishment. But for a minority that dares to walk alone, it could be the greatest blessing: they enjoy the priceless benefits of not belonging.

(1) Freedom

Being part of a group cannot only restrict the way we think and speak but our physical movement as well. Perhaps the group prohibits us from entering certain places, like buildings or even entire countries. Or we're expected to eliminate certain things from our diet because of the group's ideology and beliefs. Admittingly, many things that groups prescribe can be very beneficial for the individual's well-being. However, does that mean that we need to be part of these groups to live well?

There are many groups to belong to, from religious communities (not the religions themselves) to motorcycle gangs. But what an effort it takes to belong to these groups: to talk like they do, think as they do, dress as they do, you name it. There's no doubt that belonging to a group can be a rewarding experience, as we stand stronger together. Many are willing to make the necessary sacrifices to purchase the benefits of being part of the herd. But should you?

Not belonging to a group grants us the freedom to look how we want, dress how we want, associate with and love who we want, and think and say what we want, thus, being an ideologically independent thinker who isn't encumbered by a group's narrative. Paradoxically, this also creates the freedom to actually associate with and be part of a group of our own preference which takes you out of an unnecessary 'herd'

(2) Less in-group preference, more 'universal' love.

In Buddhism, there is a practice called *Metta*. Metta means *loving-kindness*. This loving-kindness is not selective; rather it is a universal love for all sentient beings. What we often see happening in groups is the opposite. They deeply love the members of the group, while being hostile to those that do not belong to that group. This so-called 'in-group preference' can be awesome when you are part of that group, but not so great when you aren't.

Group love is a conditional form of love because if you happen to become an outcast, this group love doesn't apply to you anymore. In-group preference challenges your freedom. Try to convert to another religion, switch to another street gang or friends' group, or support a different soccer team, and see what happens. Unfortunately, in-group preference is a human characteristic that often goes together with hostility and even violence against the out-group, including those (or especially at those) that once belonged to them. This alone is a reason not to engage with such tribalistic attitudes and stay far away from groupthink. We're all connected, and interdependent, whether we're human beings, animals, plants, or the grains of sand under our feet that allow us to walk.

If you don't belong to a certain group in the first place, you may not receive love from a selected group of people, but you don't have to restrict your love to a selected group of people either. You are free to distribute your love to whomever you want without preferences, equally, whether they're Muslims or Christians, Hell's Angels or Bandidos, and Bloods or Crips. Free from in-group preference, you can develop compassion for humanity as a whole. Or like the Buddhists do: for *all* sentient beings. I quote:

> *"Just as a mother at the risk of life loves and protects her child, her only child, so one should cultivate this boundless love for all that live in the whole universe— extending from a consciousness sublime upwards and downwards and across the world, untroubled, free from hate and enmity."*

Gautama Buddha, *Sutta Nipāta*, Mettā Sutta

(3) Self-actualization above conformity.

When I started my YouTube channel, I created a highly criticized video about an idea from pop psychology called the *'sigma male.'* The sigma male represents a male archetype that refuses to identify with a specific place in the hierarchy, or with a group for that matter. He constitutes a counterweight to the alpha, beta, delta, and omega male archetypes, which can be placed in a hierarchy: the alphas at the top, the betas at second place, and the omegas and deltas at the bottom. The sigma male stands apart as he doesn't identify with a specific place in the hierarchy. He exists outside of it. Furthermore, the sigma male uses the hierarchy to his advantage while maintaining his independence and autonomy.

There are theories about the existence of a 'sigma female' as well, and the whole alpha/beta system is generally mocked. But, in essence, the sigma character represents a person who chooses self-actualization above conformity while maintaining the skills to conform if necessary. Conformity isn't always a bad thing. In some cases, it's vital. But belonging to the herd will deprive us of time and energy, as there's no free ride in any group, and, for most people, fitting in takes effort. To quote Albert Camus: *"Nobody realizes that some people expend tremendous energy merely to be normal."*

Self-actualization terminates your dependence on others and separates you from the herd of people. Depending on one's living conditions the degree of conformity necessary to function in most modern societies is minimal. The great benefit of individualism is that as long as we abide by the law and aren't too much of a nuisance to our environment, we can pretty much live the way we want. And thus, we save energy through 'nonconformity' which we can put into self-actualization.

What Others Think

"You have no responsibility to live up to what other people think you ought to accomplish. I have no responsibility to be like they expect me to be. It's their mistake, not my failing."

Richard Phillips Feynman

It's generally a good idea to care about other people's opinions to some degree, as they *could* contain some worthwhile insight. But focusing on them too much to the point that we spend hours and hours dwelling on what people might think can leave us in agony. It's not only potentially harmful but also unnecessary. Unfortunately, most people desperately seek other people's approval, often at the cost of their own well-being.

A notoriously pessimistic German philosopher named Arthur Schopenhauer, argued in his work *The Wisdom of Life* that almost everything we devote ourselves to achieve ultimately serves to gain respect and praise from others. Just considering how far some are willing to go for a few cheers he saw it as "proof of the extent to which human folly can go." Why is it folly to care so much about what we are in the estimation of others? Because then we're letting our happiness depend on what other people think about us, which is an unreliable position to be in and takes lots of effort to maintain. Arthur Schopenhauer wrote in his work *The Wisdom of Life*:

> *"When we see that almost everything men devote their lives to attain, sparing no effort and encountering a thousand toils and dangers in the process, has, in the end, no further object than to raise themselves in the estimation of others; when we see that not only offices, titles, decorations, but also wealth, nay, even knowledge and art, are striven for only to obtain, as the ultimate goal of all effort, greater respect from one's fellowmen,—is not this a lamentable proof of the extent to which human folly can go?"*

Arthur Schopenhauer, *The Wisdom of Life*, 4.1

1) You're giving away your power.

The moment we rely on what others think about us and let our joy depend on their validation, we give away the power over our emotional states. With this attitude, it feels exhilarating when people fancy us. But when they don't, we become upset. Especially now, in the age of social media, many have made other people's approval their focal point in life. Positive attention, then, becomes a requirement for happiness, which entirely depends on the whims of those we try to impress. It can even become an addiction. Among the people we try to impress are many we don't even know. Moreover, these people tend to have ever-changing opinions, often without substance, or are downright ignorant. So why would we waste our time trying to make them like us? Chances are, we don't even like *them*? Stoic philosopher Seneca said about this:

"How mad is he who leaves the lecture room in a happy frame of mind simply because of applause from the ignorant! Why do you take pleasure in being praised by men whom you yourself cannot praise?"

Lucius Annaeus Seneca, *Moral Letters to Lucilius*, 52.11

2) It's beyond your control.

The problem with worry is that our minds try to control the uncontrollable. People's opinions are ultimately not up to us, so there isn't much we can do to stop them from disliking us. Now, this doesn't mean that we cannot *influence* what other people think. As a variation to the 'dichotomy of control (a concept from Stoicism),' professor of philosophy and author William B. Irvine proposed the 'trichotomy of control.' The dichotomy of control as presented by Epictetus distinguishes between things within our control and things outside of our control. The trichotomy of control, however, offers three categories:

(1) Things over which we have *complete control*.

(2) Things over which we have *no control at all*.

(3) And things over which we have *some* but not complete control.

Opinions of other people and what they think about us, fall into the second and third categories. In some cases, there's nothing we can do about what others think. For example, we cannot change what someone said to us in the past, and we cannot change our parents' disapproval of us when they're dead. But we *can* influence people in the present through our words and actions. But even though our attempts to make them like us could be incredibly influential, the results are still not up to us. Therefore, worrying about what's happening in the brains of others is futile, and we're better off focusing on our own actions.

3) It's a reflection of them - not you.

Often, how people react to us directly reflects how they feel themselves. When we incur hostility, indifference, or sadness as a response to our actions or even to our very presence, it may not always be personal, as they could be expressing parts of their unconscious without even realizing it. Swiss psychiatrist Carl Jung called this phenomenon 'projection'. Jung believed that people tend to repress unwanted aspects of themselves into the

30

unconscious parts of the mind, which form, what he called, *The Shadow*. As a consequence of this mechanism, we unconsciously recognize in others what we recognize in ourselves. As we dislike in others what we dislike in ourselves, an adverse emotional reaction follows, according to Jung. The popular magazine *Psychology Today* describes projection as follows, and I quote:

> *"Unconscious discomfort can lead people to attribute unacceptable feelings or impulses to someone else to avoid confronting them. Projection allows the difficult trait to be addressed without the individual fully recognizing it in themselves."*

Retrieved from *Psychology Today*, Projection, What is projection?

Jung stated that projections change the world into a replica of one's unknown face. We all see the world through a unique lens, and the unconscious plays a significant role in how we relate to our environment. Knowing this, we can put the opinions of other people into perspective.

4) You're not the center of the universe.

When we try to imagine the vastness of the universe, we begin to understand our insignificance. We may experience ourselves as the center of it all because we see it exclusively through our eyes, but most would agree that we are not. But we never know for sure. *Solipsism* is the idea that only one's mind is sure to exist, as we cannot prove that the external world, other minds included, is real. To this day, one cannot experience the existence of other minds than one's own. If *your* mind is indeed the only mind in existence, other people's opinions are nothing but illusions. Thus, nothing to make a fuss about, as they aren't real.

Even though solipsism could be the reality, there seems to be a consensus that other minds *do* exist. If the latter is the case, then other people's opinions are indeed real. But if all people have minds comparable to our own and are as immersed in their troubles as we are, then they're probably not thinking about us as much as we'd believe. Moreover, most people are concerned with what others think of *them* that they don't have time to take a good look at the very people they try to impress. In the grand scheme of things, opinions are incredibly brief and erratic, and our mistakes are quickly forgotten, along with all the times we've impressed someone. As Marcus Aurelius stated: "So many who were remembered already forgotten, and those who remembered them long gone."

5) It destroys authenticity.

Care too much about what others think and you'll turn into a sheep anxiously following the rest of the flock. As I previously explained the 'Herd mentality'. If you do as other people wish, you'll be living according to their expectations and ideals. German philosopher Friedrich Nietzsche despised the herd mentality that many people carry. He makes a distinction between the *Herren- und Sklavenmoral* (the master and slave morality). Those at the top are the strong-willed, ones who create values and rules. The many at the bottom, the herd, follow but oppose their oppressors at the *same* time. However, instead of rising to the top, those with a slave morality want others to be at their level, namely, among the other obedient, mediocre, and uniform members of the herd.

Once part of the mass, they expect you to be just like them. If you stand out, the herd sees you as evil. If you act in conflict with conventions, you may even be considered dangerous, as people usually fear the strange and unknown. Within the pack, conformity is a virtue, and authenticity is a threat. Nietzsche urges his readers to be neither a master nor a slave but to transcend this system altogether and become authentic, self-actualized people. One can only accomplish greatness if one ignores the opinions of the herd and their pre-determined virtues and unapologetically forges one's own path.

6) Life is too short.

A survey of 2,000 British adults done by the TV channel *Dave* revealed that, on average, the British spend more than six years of their lives worrying. Many of these worries concern directly or indirectly the opinions of other people. For example, 28% of Brits worry about their appearance, 21% worry about what to wear, and 17% worry about body odor on a daily basis. The average life expectancy of the British is currently 81 years old, which means that they spend 8 percent of their lives worrying. If they'd simply stop worrying about what other people think of them, they'd have about two additional years to enjoy life.

But still, even though 81 years seems quite long, it's only a fraction of time compared to humanity as a whole, let alone planet Earth. Moreover, many die young, as human life is fragile and can be taken away in the blink of an eye—what a waste of energy to spend this short and vulnerable existence wondering what other people think, isn't it? So, the fickleness and shortness of life can be a potent reminder to eliminate this destructive habit. As Seneca wrote:

> *"You live as if you were destined to live forever, no thought of your frailty ever enters your head, of how much time has already gone by you take no heed. You squander time as if you drew from a full and abundant supply, though all the while that day which you bestow on some person or thing is perhaps your last. You have all the fears of mortals and all the desires of immortals."*

7) You know yourself best.

Even though other people can provide you with valuable outside perspectives concerning your behavior, the person most knowledgeable about you is you. No matter how close we get to each other, our minds remain private spaces and often don't fully resemble what we show to the world. Carl Jung's model of the psyche differentiates several parts: the *persona*, the *ego*, the *self*, the *shadow*, and the *animus* or *anima*. Of these aspects, the persona is what we show to the world, which is just a thin layer of the self. Or, as Jung put it: "a kind of mask, designed on the one hand, to make a definite impression upon others, and on the other to conceal the true nature of the individual."

Some people can be pretty intuitive and see through the cracks of our masks; moreover, they can notice behaviors about us that we aren't even aware of. But they can *never* be sure about our true motives, secrets, and hidden personality traits because these are reserved for ourselves *only*. So, people's thoughts about us based on what they perceive often don't align with reality. Therefore, the feedback we get from others can be helpful, but the truth ultimately hides within ourselves. Deep inside, we know what we want, and the more we stay true to that, the more authentic we become, and the less we conform to what other people want us to be.

Perfect Imperfection

The pursuit of perfection has become the norm in today's world, in which chronic dissatisfaction, burnout, depression, and anxiety reign supreme. We've subjected ourselves to unrealistic standards and rigorously chase an ideal that's impossible to reach. Advertisements show us snapshots of handsome people enjoying their favorite drinks, dancing among a crowd of fashion models with ever-smiling faces. This uncompromising image of perfect happiness yells at us: "This is how your life *should* be." We try to mimic the sublimity of a lifestyle ideal as a consequence.

We spend fortunes on tweaking ourselves, our lives, and our environment, and then flood social media with pictures and videos to show the world the exquisiteness of our lives. Almost pathologically, society pursues perfection: a perfectly symmetrical face, a perfectly sculpted body, perfect hair, skin, jawline, house, friends, family, partner, children, vacations, or in short: *an existence without fault*. But this isn't only impossible *and* exhausting to pursue; it's also unnatural as far as the Japanese worldview of *wabi-sabi* is concerned.

Wabi-sabi rejects the pursuit of *perfection* and embraces the reality of *imperfection*. The philosophy behind wabi-sabi can help us escape the hamster wheel of chasing an ideal life and teaches us to appreciate existence as it is: *perfectly imperfect*.

A short history of Wabi-Sabi

The fifteenth-century Japanese ruling classes loved to display their wealth and consumed their tea from detailed Chinese cups, preferably at full moon. Zen monk Murata Shukō, however, sought to change the ceremony from a celebration of riches, into a more sober affair, by using simple Japanese-made goods. Shukō's successors further transformed the tea ceremony by simplifying the rituals and materials used, adding natural elements, and embracing the transient nature of existence. For example, instead of costly decorated ceramic cups, they used simple, old-fashioned ones, and instead of drinking at full moon, it became customary to drink at a partial or clouded moon.

The tea ceremony became a tribute to simplicity, impermanence, and imperfection. And it's considered a prominent historical example of wabi-sabi. We can also see the Buddhist elements at the core of wabi-sabi, namely the so-called three marks of existence: *impermanence*, *suffering*, and *emptiness*. Many would agree that it's impossible to achieve a clear definition of wabi-sabi. The meaning of the words "Wabi" and "Sabi" have changed over time. Nowadays, "Wabi" refers to simple things, but more in a basic, rough, imperfect, asymmetrical manner, as we find in nature. "Sabi" refers to things touched by time; that show signs of decay or damage. Yes, there's a philosophy behind it, but wabi-sabi isn't the philosophy *itself*. Perhaps, we can best describe it as an *experience*: a lucid encounter with the transient, imperfect nature of existence. An experience showing there are perfections in imperfections.

The vanity of chasing perfection

Pursuing perfection is like chasing an impossible dream. We're after a fantasy of wholeness, of an ultimate state, which we ultimately cannot attain. Some see perfection as a subjective experience, as the bar of perfection is pretty low for some people. They'll consider "perfect" what others would consider flawed. But here's the problem: what others think of as flawed *cannot* be perfect; there wouldn't be any flaws to detect if it was.

Plato argued that perfection could not exist outside of the realm of thoughts. An ideal can only exist in our minds, and the rest is just a replica. In addition to that, the transient nature of the universe and the inevitable fate of a near-perfect imitation confronts us; it falls apart eventually. A near-perfect-looking spouse? She will soon fall prey to old age. A near-perfect body? It will quickly decay. The more we try to perfect something, the more rigid and fragile it becomes, like perfectly still water is ruined by a grain of sand falling into it. Or as Lao Tzu stated.

It is easier to carry an empty cup
than one that is filled to the brim.
The sharper the knife
the easier it is to dull.
The more wealth you possess
the harder it is to protect.

Lao Tzu, *Tao Te Ching*, 9

If you keep your living room in a state of near-perfect tidiness, only a little dust is enough to ruin it. If you walk on your toes to live a near-perfect life, only a little push is enough to sweep you off your feet. Chasing perfection thus seems a fool's errand. It's an impossible goal, as we can only achieve second best, and it's difficult and eventually impossible to maintain. Therefore, chasing perfection often exhausts us, and makes us depressed, anxious, and self-loathing, as we burden ourselves with an ongoing sense of lack, of "never enough," and the fear of losing what imitation of perfection we have accomplished. It's like desperately trying to keep the water in a pond still and crystal clear, even though we cannot prevent the wind, rain, earthquakes, and other natural phenomena from shaking it up.

We, as humans, are not perfectly still, crystal clear ponds, and never will be. Most of us resemble ponds of cloudy water, subject to the whims of nature, the rains and winds of existence, and the fires of inevitable destruction. And with this fleeting, imperfect condition,

40

we resonate with the rest of the world. *Imperfection*, not perfection, is the natural state. Now, is this a tragedy? From the viewpoint of wabi-sabi, it's not. On the contrary: it's the beauty of perfect imperfection.

The embrace of imperfection

Embracing imperfection doesn't mean that we should not self-improve. Self-improvement is OK, as long as it's within reason and without the goal of perfection. Nor does it mean that we make a mess of things. A drug addiction, for instance, isn't perfectly imperfect. Instead, it's a consequence of the inability to accept life's imperfections and pain and a desperate method to banish all painful elements from one's emotional state. We could say that addicts want to experience perfection: a mental state without pain. But it's the resistance to the darker sides of life that withholds us from experiencing wabi-sabi. In Buddhist terms, this resistance leads to dissatisfaction, or *dukkha*, as we refuse to come to terms with reality, that life is inherently flawed, and that nothing we cling to remains the same. Therefore, the desire for perfection is a form of clinging: we *cling* to an idea or grand vision of how things ought to be—and clinging lies at the root of suffering. Only by letting these fantasies of perfection dissolve we can release ourselves from their torture.

Existence has no standards. No stone or tree, or mountain has to meet specific requirements. Nature simply brings these manifestations into the world before they wither and disappear. Wabi-sabi is the experience of how things are, not how they should be, in their imperfect, transient condition. "One must be deeply aware of the impermanence of the world," said Dōgen, founder of the Sōtō school of Zen Buddhism. Aging, asymmetry, crookedness, damage, decay, death: embrace them as an intrinsic part of nature, and you might begin to see the beauty in them, like the Stoic emperor Marcus Aurelius did. He described *his* wabi-sabi moment as follows:

> *"We should remember that even Nature's inadvertence has its own charm, its own attractiveness. The way loaves of bread split open on top in the oven; the ridges are just by-products of the baking, and yet pleasing, somehow: they rouse our appetite without our knowing why. Or how ripe figs begin to burst. And olives on the point of falling: the shadow of decay gives them a peculiar beauty."*

Marcus Aurelius, *Meditations*, 3.2

Living creatures are supposed to age; everything created is supposed to break. These are the natural order of things. We could ask ourselves ironically: is there anything "more perfect" than the consistently *imperfect* unfolding of nature?

How to appreciate imperfection

In the book, *Wabi Sabi: Japanese Wisdom for a Perfectly Imperfect Life,* author Beth Kempton explains the history and philosophy behind wabi-sabi and offers *practical solutions* to escape the collective pursuit of perfection and embrace imperfection. One of these solutions has to do with setting up our living environment in a perfectly imperfect way.

Wabi-sabi embraces simplicity, for example, but differently from popular forms of minimalism, which generally strive for symmetry, tidiness, and expensive furniture. The minimalism of wabi-sabi rather lies in asymmetry, not being overly tidy, and not replacing an old couch with a designer sofa, simply because it looks better. Instead, we make an inventory of the things we have, remove what we don't need, cherish what's left, and only buy something new when we truly need it. We'll end up with a not-so-perfect interior, probably with damaged furniture, chairs that don't match the couch, cracks in the walls, and tableware we've bought at a thrift shop: talk about beautiful imperfection. We can increase the wabi-sabi experience by taking nature into our homes. We can take pinecones and pieces of wood from the forest, and seashells from the beach as decorations, to create a more naturally imperfect feel.

Kempton also teaches us to see ourselves and each other in another light: not through the lens of ruthless perfectionism, but with an appreciation of flaws. We're not perfect (we're not supposed to be), nor should our goal be perfection. Instead, we're much better off accepting *who we are* and enjoying *how things are*.

> *"Put simply, wabi-sabi gives you permission to be yourself. It encourages you to do your best but not make yourself ill in pursuit of an unattainable goal of perfection. It gently motions you to relax, slow down and enjoy your life. And it shows you that beauty can be found in the most unlikely of places, making every day a doorway to delight."*

> Beth Kempton, *Wabi Sabi: Japanese Wisdom for a Perfectly Imperfect Life*

A way to practice "slowing down" is so-called *forest bathing*, in which we walk through the forest very slowly. Instead of being goal-oriented, going from point A to point B, we focus on the beauty of nature and open ourselves up to its healing capabilities. Spending time in nature is proven to reduce stress, anxiety, and worry. It helps us detach from our industrialized society full of judgment and expectation and reconnect with the vastness of the universe, welcoming us just as we are. Nature *is* perfectly imperfect and operates without judgments, without hurry, without trying to be more than it is. In nature, we find nothing but asymmetry, crookedness, and decay. Nature creates; nature destroys. Everything is in motion; nothing ever lasts. If we happen to see the beauty in all of this, we experience wabi-sabi.

You Are Enough

"I used to think the worst thing in life was to end up all alone. It's not. The worst thing in life is to end up with people that make you feel all alone."

Robin Williams

In essence, we all depend on each other. Small infants rely on their parents for survival. People with certain illnesses or the elderly for whom living depend on the aid of their fellow human beings. Grown healthy adults need others to survive and flourish; we need people to supply the supermarkets, pick up our garbage, and build infrastructure. Even those living off the grid need people; even if it's just to keep the country they're in safe. But an excessive reliance on someone else is a different story: it means that one cannot bear being alone.

People that cannot be alone continuously cling to others. Some of them are blessed with loving social circles, but others have attached themselves to people that treat them awfully. Do they really enjoy being with such people? As humans, we aren't islands. We need at least some form of social interaction to reproduce and, in many cases, to survive. However, our well-being doesn't have to depend on having romantic partners, children, or large social circles; let alone on the presence of people that aren't good for us. In many ways, social interaction can be harmful. Aside from bullying, manipulation, and exploitation by so-called 'toxic individuals', being part of a group with a certain ideology can be detrimental to our identities as individuals. We'll sacrifice our authenticity just to be part of something. Why do we do this? Is it because we want to look a part of the herd?

One of our greatest fears seems to be the fear of 'ending up alone'. That's why we stay friends with people that don't treat us well or stay in relationships tainted by domestic abuse, cheating, lying, and other destructive behaviors. People can be very abusive. Nonetheless, we feel a need to be liked by those that treat us badly. We can have hundreds of friends and feel terribly alone. Hence, we search for more friends, become more outgoing, and do our very best to impress our environment, hoping that social acceptance eventually leads to the fulfillment we're looking for. We can have thousands of followers on Instagram and as many likes on the things we post. We try to find that perfect relationship, hoping that this person makes us feel complete, which means asking our partners the impossible. How come, then, that despite our efforts we lay in our beds at night asking ourselves why we feel so unfulfilled?

I believe that the reason is two-fold. Firstly, it's because what we're looking for is already within us, and because of our pursuit to find it, we cannot see it. Secondly, our ongoing pursuits are wearing us out, and the constant people-pleasing obstructs the development of our authentic selves. We cannot achieve contentment

47

outside of ourselves. We achieve it within. No amount of money, friends, or material possessions will do the job if our contentment isn't realized internally.

Paradoxically, this contentment only reveals itself when we stop looking for it, as it appears spontaneously when we're completely immersed in the present moment, consumed by what is, without the need for anything to change, without straining ourselves to be anywhere but in the here and now. When we catch ourselves in the experience of spontaneously arisen contentment, we might want to ask ourselves if external validation is really necessary to experience it, or, if our ongoing pursuit for "likes" is actually counterproductive. We're empty because we want to be filled. But by embracing our emptiness, we eradicate this need to be filled, and, therefore, become full.

There's no doubt in my mind that socializing can lead to a lot of joy, and that there's much happiness in sharing, helping, connecting, and supporting. But there's a difference between the dependence on social interaction for the sake of one's search for completeness, and voluntary engagement with other people, without needing them to feel complete.

You are enough.

Letting Go of Material things

Simplifying Life

> *"Most of the luxuries, and many of the so-called comforts of life, are not only not indispensable, but positive hindrances to the elevation of mankind. With respect to luxuries and comforts, the wisest have ever lived a more simple and more meager life than the poor."*

Henry David Thoreau, *Walden*, Economy

Can we be happier by consuming less? Many philosophers argued that a simple life is much more fulfilling than being immersed in luxury. By consuming less, we save money, we save energy, and, we also save the most valuable asset we have as human beings: *time*. This not only allows us to experience the joys of simplicity; it's also an act of rebellion against our consumerist society.

We buy stuff that we actually don't need, depriving ourselves of hard-earned resources (even going into debt), only to further enrich an already wealthy minority. It seems that many people aren't aware of the societal brainwashing that's going on, perpetuating a sense of lack in our minds; the nagging feeling that we aren't complete, unless...x, y, and z.

Even though the consumerist society reigns supreme in all corners of the world, the human tendency to purchase more than necessary has been subject to criticism for many ages. For two years, Henry David Thoreau was an American philosopher who lived in a self-built cabin near Walden Pond where he pursued a self-sufficient life. His decision was an act of resistance against society, and part of, what he called, 'civil disobedience'. Thoreau described civil disobedience as a form of non-violent rebellion against the government. He thought that the government brings people more harm than good.

In his seclusion, Thoreau wrote his masterpiece 'Walden', in which he, among other things, describes the joys of a simple life in the midst of nature, and how he managed to survive with very little. As he wrote: "..*a man is rich in proportion to the number of things which he can afford to let alone.*" In his solitude and through his simple lifestyle, Thoreau felt "wholesome", which only further supports his criticism of overconsumption and lavish lifestyles. Admittingly, we need to consume to some extent. Some things are necessary, like food and shelter, but these are relatively easy to obtain and easy to satisfy. Epicurus once stated: *"The wealth required by nature is limited and is easy to procure, but the wealth required by vain ideals extends to infinity."*

So, what then, drives people to work overtime in jobs that they don't like, so they can buy more than they actually need? Most people are easily influenced by their environment. Trends, fashion, a guy's name on their underwear... even though we don't need those things, companies repeatedly succeed to convince us otherwise. We can feel utterly content in one moment, but experience a sense of lack in the next, because of the many voices that tell us that we need a plethora of useless junk. For a great part, people buy stuff to fit in. Or even worse: to prevent that others won't look down on them. In some communities, you just cannot afford not to have at least a mid-size car and a 4-bedroom house.

> *"What fools these mortals be! They allow the cheapest and most useless things, which can easily be replaced, to be charged in the reckoning, after they have acquired them; but they never regard themselves as in debt when they have received some of that precious commodity, – time! And yet time is the one loan that even a grateful recipient cannot repay."*

Lucius Annaeus Seneca, *Moral Letters to Lucilius*, 1.3

Time is our most valuable asset, and it's running out as you read. We can exchange time for money, but we cannot exchange money for time. Yet, we waste our lives in the pursuit of keeping up with the Joneses. Or as Fight Club's main character Tyler Durden states: *"...working jobs we hate so we can buy shit we don't need."* The consequence is that (and I paraphrase Durden here) the stuff you own ends up owning you. It becomes a burden, a deadweight, something that costs us more than it brings us. So, what does it bring us? Status, respect, praise, short-term pleasure? These things are completely beyond our control and unnecessary for experiencing contentment.

Ultimately, the companies that persuade us to consume aren't really the problem. These are *external* forces that are not up to us. The problem lies in us allowing ourselves to be manipulated. The root of this weakness lies in *fear*. Alain de Botton described a phenomenon of modern society called 'status anxiety' as *"the constant tension or fear of being perceived as 'unsuccessful' by the society in materialistic terms."* Most people of our time have probably some form of status anxiety.

So, what's the solution? Caring less about what other people think is probably a good starter. Friends that only accept us because of our status and material success aren't really friends, are they? Moreover, what's there to be gained from impressing people we don't even know just for the sake of impressing them? Are people ridiculing us because we don't measure up to their definition of success? Well, that's *their* business; not ours, I'd say. Once we accept that our wholeness does not depend on material success, we can truly enjoy the richness of a simple life. As Lao Tzu, author of the *Tao Te Ching* once wrote: *"those who know they have enough are truly wealthy."*

A simple life doesn't mean that we must ascetically renounce everything material. Besides the basic necessities, there's value in things that serve us in the practical sense. Ours is the ability to discern between necessity, practicality, and luxury, so we prevent ourselves to become prisoners of our possessions. Being content with little is the ultimate *civil disobedience* in modern times. It loosens the grip that society has over us, by *not needing* what they have to offer in exchange for our time and labor. By owning and needing less, our existence becomes less *complicated* and less *stressful*.

A life of simplicity grants us the space to truly enjoy the time that's given to us, to spend our time on what we deem as important. As Thoreau stated: *"Our life is frittered away by detail ... simplify, simplify!"*

Minimalism

One day, the legendary Chinese recluse Xu You watched a mole drinking water from a pond. He realized that the mole, when thirsty, only drinks a bellyful: no more, no less, but exactly the quantity it needs. The mole doesn't encumber itself with excesses, because that would only impede its movement; unlike humans, who often tend to consume much more than they need. We may not drink *water* in excess, but we often overburden ourselves with all kinds of material possessions, buying much more than we need to stay alive and thriving.

Consumerism comes *with a price* as well, as it requires resources to keep up with the other consumers. Therefore, many people are willing to work themselves into an early grave dedicating their lives to accumulate what we could call 'extensions of themselves', extensions of their egos. "I have more, so I am more," they tend to think, so by increasing their possessions they increase their sense of self. But there's a countermovement to our consumerist society, known as *minimalism*. Minimalists are people who turn their backs to overconsumption and decide to live with no more than necessary ultimately simplifying their lives.

Aside from it being a lifestyle trend today, minimalism is a concept that people have been practicing for centuries. There's a sense of freedom in simplicity, and not owning much, which many sages and philosophers have experienced throughout the ages. They saw that possessions don't define *who we are* and that the ongoing pursuit of external things prevents us from experiencing life to the fullest.

Minimalism: the 'wrong' way

Minimalism can be interpreted in different ways. Essentially it points to living with the bare essentials, reducing the clutter in our lives, and refraining from overextending ourselves. In other words: *to keep it simple.* But there are certain modes of minimalism that slightly miss the mark. First of all, there's extreme asceticism, which is geared towards going *below* the minimum. For example, it's said that when prince Siddhartha Gautama lived as an ascetic he only ate one grain of rice a day, and hardly had any flesh left on his bones.

In a way, consuming *below* one's needs is a very 'minimalistic' thing to do, as it hardly requires consumption. Also, such a way of life goes together with the renunciation of possessions, which leads to a simple life. But in the case of the extreme ascetic, less isn't more, but truly less, as it's a road to self-destruction. Siddhartha Gautama concluded that the punishment of the body won't lead to enlightenment. So, he quit the ascetic lifestyle before he became the Buddha.

Second of all, there's a fashionable, wealthy form of minimalism, which focuses more on getting rid of unnecessary, and often, 'cheap' objects, while maintaining a selection of very expensive things. For example, a minimalistic living room in a two-million-dollar apartment. In this case, minimalism is still used as a means to display wealth, as the absence of cheap, obsolete objects *accentuates* the expensive things we do have. Thus, we can see this as a sophisticated form of consumerism, as it still revolves around status and possessions, and thus, one still needs a lot of money to obtain and sustain this lifestyle.

Such a stance goes at the expense of the true power behind minimalist living, which is that our *baseline happiness* (or contentment) is achieved with a minimal amount of resources, and is detached from the burden of status and extreme wealth. But this idea is difficult to accept when the basic ideology of our consumerist culture is that *less is less*, and *more is more*. This has everything to do with how we collectively value social status. And that social status isn't measured by one's virtue or spirituality, but by the car one drives, the house one lives in, the furniture one possesses, and the clothes one wears. What we *have* seems to determine our place in the dominance hierarchy.

So, in a society in which holiness is wealth, the church is the shopping mall, and prayer is consumption, those who dare to reject these 'sacred elements' will be regarded as blasphemers. Nevertheless, the joy of simple living can far outweigh the negatives.

The joys of not having

Emperor Yao regarded the recluse Xu You with the utmost respect; so much that he was willing to give up his throne to him. However, Xu You (who lived a solitary and quiet life by the riverside) refused, telling the emperor that he did not need "all under heaven", and said to him: "When the tailorbird builds her nest in the deep wood, she uses no more than one branch."

The story about Xu You can be found in an ancient Chinese text attributed to the Taoist philosopher Zhuangzi. The recluse who lives in poverty gets handed something that many people can only dream of, which is a whole empire under his command. But the story tells us that he chose to live as a hermit in a solitary place. Xu probably realized that power comes with great responsibility and that ruling an empire will not allow him to live a simple, quiet life.

The less you own, the less you can lose, and the less you have to worry about. Lao Tzu wrote the following passage in the Tao Te Ching:

> *If you overvalue possessions, people will begin to steal.*
> *Do not display your treasures or people will become envious.*

Lao Tzu, *Tao Te Ching*, 3

Having lots of possessions requires adequate protection. That's why we see that outwardly rich people often live in fear, hidden behind walls in gated communities. By not owning much, on the other hand, we save a lot of time and energy. We don't have to look after our expensive things and they don't distract us either. And we're still able to find joy in the world, as we don't have to *own* what we enjoy.

Why do we need a 1000 square feet garden, if we can go for a walk in the woods? Why do we need a 6-bedroom mansion if we can live in a small cheap house, and enjoy the world outside for free? This is what American transcendentalist philosopher Henry David Thoreau must have thought as well when he decided to live in a cabin in the woods near Walden pond. Thoreau deliberately chose a simple life because he believed that this could lead to spiritual growth. In essence, a minimalist life facilitates equanimity. When the living expenses are low, we don't have to work like dogs and can spend more time enjoying the world around us, with a sense of contentment; this joy of not needing anything more than this moment has to offer. Isn't that what *freedom* is all about?

Defining our needs

So, what do we truly need? Where lies the golden middle path between asceticism and consumerism that a minimalist is looking for? In the course of history, there have been several philosophers who shaped their minimalist lifestyle in their unique ways. Take, for example, Diogenes the Cynic who lived in a barrel without possessions. The story goes that for a while he owned a drinking cup, which he threw away when he saw a child drinking from his hands, and remarked: "A child has beaten me in plainness of living." Aside from that, Diogenes didn't have shame, and couldn't care what people thought about him. His state of detachment from worldly goods as well as other people's opinions made him invincible; no one could hurt him.

But, for those who don't fancy living in a barrel on the streets, and rather live a more integrated life that doesn't make you into an outcast, there's a more practical recipe for minimalist living, which was invented by a philosopher named Epicurus. Epicurus created a hierarchy of needs, that shows us which desires we should pursue and which we shouldn't. Natural and necessary desires like food, shelter, and human connection, are the ones we should focus on. Moreover, these natural desires are generally easily obtainable and also have natural limits, which means that they're satiable. The desires that we should avoid, he called 'vain and empty' desires, which include power, wealth, and fame. These desires he considered unnecessary, unnatural, and impossible to satisfy as they don't have a natural limit. Epicurus also urged us to cherish what we *do* have and stop focusing on what we lack. Or as he stated: "do not spoil what you have by desiring what you have not; remember that what you now have was once among the things you only hoped for."

There's great joy in having little. As opposed to the lives of those seeking to consume to infinity, painfully exchanging their very lives for boosting their self-esteem, so they feel accepted in a world where the amount of stuff we have is how we define how worthy we are. For a minimalist, this is the very *definition* of a miserable life. In minimalism, one lets go of the conventional ideas of wealth and status, knowing that true wealth lies within and social status is not only an unnecessary luxury; it's also difficult to obtain, easy to lose, and, for a great part, out of our control. Instead, minimalists choose to live simply, as they know that the ability to let go of all these worldly goods is where the true wealth lies; the joy of a simple, easy life. For them, simplicity is the ultimate form of sophistication. As Thoreau stated:

"I am convinced, both by faith and experience, that to maintain one's self on this earth is not a hardship but a pastime if we live simply and wisely."

Henry David Thoreau

Abundance

Imagine that we need one million dollars to be happy. If that's the case, then as long as we don't reach this amount, we're unhappy. If we look at humanity's poverty and its small percentage of millionaires, we can then conclude that happiness is scarce if it requires seven figures in a bank account. Nevertheless, suppose we deeply desire to be happy and feel incomplete as long as we don't reach this mental state. So far, we've managed to save a hundred thousand dollars, which might be a lot of money to most of us, but if we take the requirement of happiness we've set for ourselves into account, we are nine hundred thousand dollars in debt. It's not comfortable to be in debt, as it weighs heavily on our shoulders and implies a state of *owing* something, which, in this case, is a desire left unpaid. Only if we obtain what we want is this debt paid off. If what we need is scarce, it's challenging to get and easy to lose because everyone wants it. In our experience, then, *happiness* is in short supply.

Suppose we let our life satisfaction depend on things challenging to obtain. In that case, we set ourselves up for stress, discontent, and insecurity. We tend to worry a lot about not having what we want, losing what we have, and the future not playing out as we desire. An alternative would be a minimalist mindset of *abundance*. If we experience no shortage in getting our needs met, we'll quickly achieve a state of contentment. And the quickest way to reach abundance is by downgrading our needs. The less you want, the more you have. And when we have plenty, we care less about gain and loss; we're less stressed about missing out and less fearful of change.

From scarcity to abundance

When happiness is in short supply, we need to work hard to obtain it. The requirements for happiness we've decided for ourselves could be material possessions, money, high social status, a near-perfect partner, or, perhaps, a combination of these factors. Imagine slaving away endlessly to meet these requirements while continually experiencing this nagging sense of dissatisfaction (because as long as our needs aren't satisfied, we're not happy). Imagine that when we finally obtain our holy grail, we anxiously hold on to it, as losing what we've worked so hard for would mean the end of our happiness. What a demanding life that would be.

The more specific our conditions for happiness are, the more difficult it becomes to be satisfied. Especially when we've made our happiness dependent on outside circumstances that are incredibly fickle; even the smallest of changes threaten the foundations of our well-being. An example of this would be a person who desires a "perfect life," which entails a "perfect" house, "perfect" family, "perfect" job, "perfect" social circle, and the list goes on. Satisfaction requires all variables to be fulfilled.

But if one of them isn't "perfect," then this person's sense of happiness collapses like a house of cards.

As the backward law (see chapter *The Backwards Law*) shows us: the more we *need* to be satisfied, the less satisfied we become; and the more we want, the less we feel we have. So, the less we need from the world, the more we'll experience abundance. Abundance implies that we have more than enough. But what's enough? That's subjective: for some, it's never enough. For others, very little is enough. Also, our idea of what's enough tends to change over time. For example, when we're still in college, having enough money to buy food and go to parties tends to be enough. But when we're advanced in our careers, we could very well be dissatisfied with salaries that dwarf the income of most students. The conclusion is that the idea of abundance depends on our vision and our thinking.

The good news is that we can *change* our perceptions of what's enough. And the less we need to have enough, the easier we're satisfied. We're also less distressed by the fickleness of the outside world, as a changing environment won't easily affect what's plentiful. Just look at the oceans; despite all the changes our planet has gone through during the last four billion years, they're still around.

Imagine someone happy and fulfilled with the essentials, like clothing, food, shelter, and a few people to talk to, now and then, online or offline. This person's satisfaction depends on abundant things and, thus, is easy to attain. So, it's tough to harm this person's contentment because what's abundant will always be readily available, contrary to what's scarce. So, the less we need, the stronger our position becomes. However, we can't be without desire entirely. Having needs is part of being human. But we can manage our desires, so we dwell less frequently in a realm of scarcity and lack and predominantly in the domain of abundance. As Epicurus once stated: "If you want to make a man happy, add not unto his riches but take away from his desires." Let's explore a couple of ways to channel our desires so that we can shift from scarcity to abundance and simplify our lives.

The power of moderation

Epicurus distinguished three kinds of desires: *natural and necessary desires* (like food, shelter, and rest), *natural and unnecessary desires* (like luxurious food and expensive clothing), and *vain desires* (like power, extreme wealth, and fame). In short, Epicurus believed that we should focus on the first (which are necessary and easy to satisfy) and avoid the latter (which are unnecessary and impossible to satisfy).

Epicurus' taxonomy leaves a vast grey area of needs that, in the modern world, aren't necessary for happiness but are still abundant and, thus, easy to obtain.

65

We can consider listening to music, playing video games, or browsing YouTube among these things. Looking at the amount of music, games, and videos available these days, we could say that these pleasures are abundant. But we tend to overindulge in them. Overindulgence is problematic because to attain satisfaction we need more and more, as our senses become less sensitive and need more stimulation. The more we need, the less abundance we'll experience. Playing a video game for eight hours in a row may not be enough anymore; we need longer, more stimulating sessions.

If we'd choose our needs wisely, we might not want to engage with them in ways that disempower us. The Stoics proposed a virtue called 'moderation' to curb our desires, so they do not rule us. Moderation includes *modesty* and *self-control*. If we master these virtues, then pleasures in abundant supply will not conquer us but serve us only when we choose, so they maintain their quality of being plentiful *and* enjoyable.

Being thankful for what we have

Humans tend to focus on what they want rather than on what they have. But doing so means we exchange potential sources of contentment for unfulfilled desires and the pain that comes with that. The things we have are a very accessible source of joy. Is there anything easier to obtain than what we already have? Is there anything more acutely available than what's already in our possession? When we fail to cherish what we have, we'll be dissatisfied, so we need to put in the effort to look for something else. But if we turn away from what we *don't* have and start focusing on what we *do* have, happiness will be a bargain.

Being grateful for what we have increases the *value* of what we have. Gratitude can help you to minimize your needs and let go of material things. For example, many people view the houses they live in as insufficient: too small, too old, and too ugly. But they could also see the glass as half-full: they have a roof over their heads, live small but cozily, and old doesn't always mean unsuitable for living. Even though larger, newer, better-looking houses are available, the places they live in still suit their basic need: shelter. There are many people with worse living spaces, or even without homes. Compared to them, any home is a blessing and something to be grateful for. When we shift the paradigm from dissatisfaction to gratitude, the value of our current house increases; we now value and cherish what we previously devalued. Gratitude, therefore, is not just a free-of-charge ticket to satisfaction; it's also a way to save money. Had we satisfied the desire for a new house, we would have eventually ended up with the same level of satisfaction, but we also pay most dearly for it.

Contemplating the price of our needs

Our needs come with a price. In general, what's abundant is cheap and what's scarce is expensive. And it's easier to acquire something affordable than something lavish. But still, the level of difficulty depends on our context. Someone wealthy, for example, has an easy time obtaining a costly watch, which, for a poor person, could take years of saving money. Even though the watch's price remains the same, it's relatively cheaper for the rich than for the poor. So, when selecting our needs, it's wise to contemplate what they truly cost us. American philosopher Henry David Thoreau had a simple rule for this: "The price of anything is the amount of life you exchange for it."

Whenever we desire something, we could immediately ask ourselves: what amount of life will I exchange for this? How many hours of work does this purchase require of me? And how much does this work affect my health? Things that need a *small* amount of life in exchange can be considered cheap. Items that require a large amount of life can be regarded as expensive. If we focus on the needs that are cheap and easy to fulfill, we experience abundance. This abundance is either based on having plenty of resources or the minor requirement of life satisfaction necessary to fulfill it. Taking an expensive mortgage may not be such a great idea if this requires us to walk on our toes for it. Even though we might buy a dream house, eventually, the price could outweigh the benefit.

Staying out of long-term debt

Being in debt can be a very stressful experience, as an obligation to pay off what we owe shackles us. Although we associate debt with money, our desires also generate debt to one of the most tormenting, nagging, demanding creditors we can think of: the mind. How is the mind a creditor? Every time we notice that a desire arouses within us, we're instantly in debt. We moved from the debt-free experience of contentment, in which we owe ourselves nothing as we have no desires need to be paid off, into the red. The mind demands that we fulfill this desire, and if we don't, it keeps knocking on our door like a debt collector. To a certain extent, this is inevitable. When we're hungry, for example, we must satisfy our hunger with food. When we're tired and in need of rest, we must pay off this debt by sleeping. But in most parts of the world, food and sleep are widely available. So, paying off these natural desires isn't hard to do.

Real difficulties arise when we immerse ourselves in long-term desires that we must fulfill to feel satisfied. By doing this, we burden ourselves with long-term debt: a feeling of lack that only goes away when this desire is fulfilled, which can leave us feeling incomplete for a long time. An example of such a predicament is how some people handle unrequited love. Imagine having romantic feelings for someone, but this person doesn't feel the same way about you. If you're unable to accept this and spend your days hoping that this person someday reciprocates, you've set yourself up for long-term dissatisfaction. Your mind has turned the romantic interest of someone who's *not* interested into a prerequisite for happiness. So, you'll be in debt until the mind gets what it wants, which probably never happens. Hope, therefore, is not a good strategy for happiness.

Instead of letting our *happiness* depend on realizing dreams and desires in the future, especially those that take ages to realize (or we never realize at all), we might want to focus on finding joy in more readily available things. Enjoying the immediate doesn't mean that we shouldn't have long-term goals, but that we appreciate the small things and don't let our joie de vivre solely depend on realizing the big.

We *can* generate satisfaction with very little, with what's abundant. But this often means that instead of conquering the world, we need to conquer our *desire* for the world. Ultimately, there are two ways of creating abundance. The first one is by accumulating more of what we desire, but by doing so, we become dependent on outside circumstances that we cannot control. The second one is by putting a chain on our desires, so we make the things that are already here, in the present, more satisfying to us. The less we desire from the world, the more abundant the world appears. Leaving our materialistic non-essential needs and focusing on what we actually need satisfies our inner selves. Thus, the less you want, the more you have.

Keeping It Simple

Epicurus believed that we don't need all these extravagant pleasures to be happy. Expensive luxurious vacations to distant places, accumulating an excessive amount of money and possessions, or acquiring power through politics will not lead us to satisfaction in the long run. If anything, such pursuits only make us crave for more and deprive us of time, energy, and, in some cases, our morality. Epicurus himself chose a simple life, enjoying weak wine, bread, and cheese, and discussing philosophy with friends.

The chapter 'Minimalism' attempted to define a philosophical outlook on minimalism. People use the word 'minimalism' in different contexts. In music, it's a style characterized by simplicity. There's minimalistic art that uses only simple and abstract forms. And recently, there's been a surge in people adopting minimalism as a lifestyle by minimizing their possessions to get rid of unnecessary clutter. These forms of minimalism seem to have one common denominator: they use the *minimal* to achieve a goal, whether it's a nice piece of music or art or a pleasant living environment. But could we apply this principle to our overall well-being as well? How can we live happy, prosperous lives without breaking the bank? How can we be satisfied without cost? How can we be wealthy with only the bare minimum? Several philosophers of the past shed their light on questions like these.

The poverty of the rich

Having lots of money and material possession doesn't necessarily make someone rich. Often, but not always, wealthy people crave to accumulate more while being afraid of losing what they have. They live with stress, and mistrust of others, and, sometimes, are entirely isolated from the masses who aren't financially well off. These people may successfully accumulate material wealth, but, in many cases, this doesn't happen without significant sacrifice. For example, someone working eighty hours a week hardly has time to relax, and there's only a little time left to spend with family and friends, the latter Epicurus believed to be one of the essential sources of well-being.

Moreover, according to a study in the *American Journal of Industrial Medicine*, consistently working more than 40 hours a week is detrimental to our health, as the risk of coronary heart disease increases significantly. Another study, published in the *Journal of Occupational and Environmental Medicine*, found that working more than 45 hours a week (for at least ten years) was associated with an increased risk of cardiovascular disease. Of course, not all rich people overwork, and not all people who overwork are rich. But there's a correlation.

73

A book named *The Way of Chuang Tzu* written by Thomas Merton contains a series of the author's own versions of Zhuangzi's classic sayings. The Taoist philosopher observed how the world values "money, reputation, long life, and achievement." The world condemns "lack of money, a low social rank, a reputation of being no good, and an early death." More than two millennia later, nothing has changed. As Zhuangzi stated back then, people seek things the world values and avoid what it condemns. And if they're deprived of what they seek, they experience panic and despair.

> *"They are so concerned for their life that their anxiety makes life unbearable, even when they have the things they think they want. Their very concern for enjoyment makes them unhappy. The rich make life intolerable, driving themselves in order to get more and more money which they cannot really use. In doing so, they are alienated from themselves and exhaust themselves in their own service as though they were slaves of others."*

Zhuangzi (interpreted by Thomas Merton), *The Way of Chuang Tzu*, Perfect Joy

And so, Zhuangzi seems to have pointed out significant downsides to the concept of working hard to play hard. Is the playing worth the work? If not, and we choose not to chase what the world values, are we then condemned to a life of misery? Or can we perhaps find cheaper pleasures that provide the same satisfaction?

The cheapest pleasures

Some people would argue that the American transcendentalist philosopher Henry David Thoreau was a minimalist. He lived at Walden pond in a small cabin for two years, with only the necessities, like a bed, a desk, a table, and a few chairs. On March 11th, 1856, Thoreau described in his journal a contempt for wealth and traveling compared to the simple life and the streams, woods, and natural phenomena he encounters in his own village. He figured that if he'd let himself get used to luxury, distant travel, or the tastes of fine wine or brandy, then *those* things become more and more to him, and the simple things less and less. He'd need expensive pleasure to satisfy his needs.

As an example, Thoreau stated that exchanging the city of Paris for his native village would be a "wretched bargain." And yes: the hassle and the increased cost of living are consequences of developing a taste for things beyond our necessities. The easily accessible enjoyment may then move to the background and may be considered uninteresting, boring, and insufficient to satisfy our needs. We got ourselves 'hooked' on expensive pleasures, which also come with higher prices.

Furthermore, some people may be hooked explicitly on the idea that the things they enjoy are supposed to be 'expensive.' The actual pleasure these things provide is secondary.

Thoreau stuck to the most common events and everyday phenomena, like what his senses perceived during his daily walks, conversations with his neighbors, and the sight of marsh hawks in Concord meadows. He wrote:

> *"In this sense, I am not ambitious. I do not wish my native soil to become exhausted and run out through neglect. Only traveling is good which reveals to me the value of a home and enables me to enjoy it better. That man is the richest whose pleasures are the cheapest."*

Henry David Thoreau, Early Spring in Massachusetts

We could say that the wealthiest person isn't the one who has the most but the one most satisfied with what he has. And that being full of desires to be fulfilled is poor, but being content is rich. "If thou wilt makes a man happy, add not unto his riches but take away from his desires," Epicurus once said. But what *are* these cheap pleasures Thoreau speaks about? How can we enjoy life with minimal cost?

There are different ideas on what cheap pleasure entails, as 'pleasure' is different for everyone, and whether or not something is cheap depends on one's circumstances. The 19th-century author, geologist, and evolutionary thinker Robert Chambers, for example, stated in a journal that 'reading' is an inexpensive way of deriving pleasure:

> *"Reading, in fact, is nowadays almost as free as air. It would thus appear that all the best pleasures are the cheapest. Nature seems to tell us that we have only to restrain our wishes to what is good, and pure, and elevating, in order to be satisfied without cost."*

Robert Chambers, *Chamber's Journal (Volume 6)*, Things which are to be got for little or nothing.

Chamber's suggestion is in line with Arthur Schopenhauer's views on pleasure. In one of his essays, he argued that the highest pleasures are the pleasures of sensibility, or "intellectual" pleasures, such as thought, a taste for poetry, learning, reading, and meditation. According to Schopenhauer, all other pleasures (that are not of the intellect) are of a lower kind. They're always satisfied at the cost of pain. Intellectual pleasures are often very cheap. Those who enjoy them can consider living in today's day and age a blessing, as food for the intellect is widely available and basically free of cost.

However, what Schopenhauer calls 'lower' pleasures can nevertheless be cheap. For example, enjoying a nice meal doesn't have to be expensive if you cook it yourself, especially when it's a simple meal, which Epicurus would endorse. The price of walking is 'muscular energy,' but not too much, and is, aside from that, an activity free of charge.

The best of them all

What pleasure is most enjoyable but also very affordable? Epicurus may have an answer to that question. His philosophy distinguished moving pleasures from static pleasures. Moving pleasures involve activities to satisfy one's desire, like eating in a restaurant when hungry. Static pleasures, however, occur when a desire is satisfied. For example, the moment one isn't hungry anymore.

According to Epicurus, the highest pleasures are the *passive* pleasures, in other words, the lack of discomfort or, simply, contentment. Like Schopenhauer's view on pleasure, Epicurus thought that 'moving pleasures' take a lot of effort. Pursuing them could also be dangerous. Of course, the degree of effort and danger depends on the pleasure itself. For example, opening the fridge and taking out some food doesn't take a lot of effort, and most of the time isn't very dangerous. But traveling around the world requires us to earn and save a lot of money, go from place to place, negotiate with people, and keep ourselves safe in foreign areas.

Static pleasure, on the other hand, takes no effort at all. It's simply the feeling of contentment after our needs are satisfied. Schopenhauer, in turn, recognizes that happiness consists, for the most part, of "peace of mind and contentment." But to achieve this, we need to reduce a strong impulse of human nature, which he called the 'will to live.' And that's challenging to do, as it requires a degree of asceticism that probably isn't reserved for the vast majority of humankind.

How do we achieve static pleasure? Is there a way to be content as often as possible without becoming an ascetic? If Thoreau, Chambers, Schopenhauer, Zhuangzi, and Epicurus were still alive, they would've possibly agreed that satiating ourselves through simple, affordable pleasures is our best bet. Such pleasures are easy to come by and widely available; making them the source of our enjoyment saves us from the stress we'd experience if only what's scarce and expensive would satisfy our needs. The cheaper our pleasures of choice, the less time and effort we need to attain them, and the more we enjoy not wishing for anything else. If that isn't the ultimate form of minimalism, then what is?

Letting Go of People

Missing Someone

Most of us have been in a position in which we had to say goodbye to someone dear to us. This could be because of the cycle of life and death, but also because of a breakup or being separated from friends by moving to another country. When we're strongly attached to someone, the separation can hurt a lot and often goes together with feelings of nostalgia and grief. Here are four ideas from philosophy that could be helpful to cope with missing someone.

(1) Contemplate impermanence.

It strikes me how many people long for permanence in an impermanent universe; especially in regard to other people. When a situation feels good, we wish to remain in it as long as possible. So, if we're attached to our loved ones, we do not want these bonds to ever end. The reality is that everything comes and goes, including the people dear to us. Although the reality of impermanence may be a source of grief, it also, quite paradoxically, allowed for our loved ones to exist in the first place. Moreover, impermanence makes life appealing.

Imagine that the presence of our loved ones is permanent; that they've always been here and never cease to exist. They are never born and never die. They would've been unchanging, static, and completely predictable. What's the appeal of that? Humans generally aren't attracted to the unchanged and predictable. What attracts humans, as far as I've observed, is uncertainty. Uncertainty is mysterious, interesting, and exciting. In a relationship with another person, we bond in the face of complete unpredictability. Will we remain together until the end or part within a few years? No one knows, and that's what makes it worthwhile.

The nature of change means that people change. They change interests, change preferences, change the places they live, age, get sick and die. Trying to resist such changes is fighting a losing battle. A wiser approach would be to fully enjoy our loved ones now they're present while accepting that, one day, Fate removes them from our lives and we need to let them go.

> *"If we are not empty, we become a block of matter. We cannot breathe, we cannot think. To be empty means to be alive, to breathe in, and to breathe out. We cannot be alive if we are not empty. Emptiness is impermanence, it is change. We should not complain about impermanence, because without impermanence, nothing is possible."*

Thich Nhat Hanh

(2) Remove entitlement.

Life doesn't come with any guarantees. The universe has given us what we have and we aren't entitled to anything more than what's coming to us. This may sound a bit harsh, but nature has never promised us things like long-lasting stable marriages, visually appealing bedpartners, larger-than-life wealth, or giant social circles. Perhaps society makes us believe that we deserve a number of things in our lives but reality teaches us that we don't.

When we miss someone, we are dissatisfied with the situation of not having this person in our lives. Especially after a breakup, we sometimes feel that we have a 'right' to be with that person. Their absence disturbs us. But in the grand scheme of things, we don't 'own' people – it's simply our turn to be with them. Some stick around for life, but the majority are just passengers. According to Stoic philosopher Epictetus we should treat life as a dinner party, by simply enjoying what we get from it, but accept the things that pass us by.

"Is anything brought around to you? Put out your hand and take your share with moderation. Does it pass by you? Don't stop it. Has it not yet come? Don't stretch your desire towards it, but wait till it reaches you. Do this with regard to children, to a wife, to public posts, to riches, and

you will eventually be a worthy partner of the feasts of the gods."

Epictetus, *Enchiridion*, 15

(3) Love them without being physical with them.

Loving someone means setting them free. When people walk out of our lives (or are in any other way separated from us), instead of wishing them to return for our own pleasure, we could also love them selflessly. If we only love people because of what they can do for us, which can be something as simple as keeping us company, then we might miss them partly because we miss their utility in our lives. They made us feel good, they cooked us nice meals, they listened to our rants, and they entertained us. And now that's all gone, we feel dissatisfied.

We could ask ourselves: *what's best for them?* Was walking away from us in their best interest? Did they, for example, move to another country to pursue their dreams and ambitions? Thus, what's in it for them, instead of what's in it for us? Chances are that they are better off now, and that should be a reason to be happy for them. And if they aren't, we can at least wish them the best, even if we're not with them (and not 'getting' anything out of them). This way, we might transform the painful desire for them to be with us, into what the Buddhists call *Metta*:

an unconditional wish for all living beings to be well, safe, and happy.

(4) Focus on the present moment.

Hands down the most direct way to deal with missing someone is to move your attention to the present. When we, for example, focus on the task at hand or immerse ourselves in a conversation with people our focus will not be on the person we miss.

> *"Then remind yourself that past and future have no power over you. Only the present—and even that can be minimized. Just mark off its limits. And if your mind tries to claim that it can't hold out against that... well, then, heap shame upon it."*

Marcus Aurelius, *Meditations*, 8.36

When we spend large amounts of time and energy on missing someone, we hand over *the power over our mood* to past memories. Not that there's anything wrong with memories, but should the desire for what's already gone dictate what we do today? In this case, we'll never be able to let go. If we can't let go and long for something that isn't there, our present-day appears gray and lifeless, often full of despair. By opening the door to the past, waiting in vain for it to walk back in, the door to the present simultaneously closes. This results in wasted opportunities. If we miss someone, and really love that person, and this love is mutual: don't you think that this person would want the best for us, which is living well in the present moment?

Fake Love

Falling in love is the insanity of the soul. Anyone who's ever fallen in love knows that it's one of the most intense experiences that a human being can have. More often than not, logic and reason are thrown overboard because the person of our desire seems to have enchanted every cell in our body, and there's nothing we want more than to *be* with that person. It's dangerous, exciting, crazy, unpredictable, and, when we're truly affected by it, completely out of control. Philosophers throughout the ages have been fascinated by this phenomenon.

Søren Kierkegaard was a Danish philosopher from the nineteenth century. During his studies at the University of Copenhagen, he met the nine years younger Regine Olsen. He fell head over heels in love with her and this feeling was mutual. But for Kierkegaard, this event seemed *tragic* rather than *beautiful*. Kierkegaard distinguished different types of love. 'Passionate preferential love', he regarded as just another form of self-love. Because this type of love says more about what *we* are attracted to, and how the object of our desire can gratify our needs, instead of what we can actually give without expecting something in return. When we fall in love with someone, isn't it so that we're attracted to this person because she has the ability to evoke a sense of pleasure in *ourselves*, and that this pleasure is more about how this particular human being makes us *feel* than the human being itself?

As opposed to preferential love, Kierkegaard distinguished what he called 'non-preferential love', which is not fueled by passion, is non-erotic, and is not selfish. Instead, it seems to come from a place of equanimity and can be given away endlessly, as it is a boundless source that we all have access to. He described this kind of love as the love we have for a neighbor, no matter who this person happens to be, instead of someone of our preference.

> *"Neighbor" presses as closely as possible upon the selfishness in life. If there are only two men, the other man is the neighbor; if there are millions, each one of these is the neighbor, who is again closer to one than "the friend" and "the beloved," insofar as those, as being the objects of preferential love, gradually become analogous to the self-love in one.*

Soren Kierkegaard, *Works of Love*, p. 19 (translated by H. Hong & E. Hong)

Because Kierkegaard saw through the veil of passion, he knew that the intense love between him and Regine was not sustainable, and would eventually fade away. A year after they engaged, he broke the engagement. He wept, and grieved, but accepted his self-imposed destiny as a solitary writer and remained emotionally faithful to Regine. Regine, however, married another man, but never completely *let go* of Søren. At least, so they say. The beauty of this is that by breaking the engagement, Kierkegaard immortalized his deep love for Olsen, as she remained very influential and almost became a mythological archetype throughout his life.

Kierkegaard's preferential love comes with strong attachments and is - when aimed at a lover - drenched with lust. In its insanity, it produces a chaotic explosion of contradicting emotions; from great longing to extreme anger and jealousy. Why in the world should we pursue something that can change from affection to hate at the flip of a switch? Is this true love? Or is it a curse? Is it a manifestation of inner madness that's been elevated to the domain of the sacred?

When we look at ancient philosophy, we discover that Kierkegaard wasn't the only one that questions what we hold in such high regard as a species: *romantic love*. In Buddhism, romantic love is recognized as *potentially* harmful. This means that the love between two people doesn't necessarily have to be *true* love; especially when it involves unhealthy attachment and suffering.

> *"If romantic love is true love, it can also bring a lot of happiness. But if it is not true love, it will make you suffer, and make the other suffer as well."*

Now, this may seem obvious. But how many times does the experience of falling in love goes accompany deep desire and the pain that flows from it? The ancient Stoics already observed back then that the problem with desire is a disappointment when one fails to obtain the object of his desire. This leads to jealousy, possessiveness, and ownership. When two people are deeply in love with each other and wouldn't mind being handcuffed together, they also produce a fear of separation, which is a form of suffering.

Tragic hero Anakin Skywalker (from the Star Wars films) serves as an example of the destructive nature of romantic love, as his fear of losing Padmé controlled him almost completely. This fear, this deep desire to never be separated from her as he was separated from his mother, made him easily exploitable by evil. Anakin sacrifices the true, altruistic love required as a Jedi, for selfish and preferential love, regardless of the death and misery he creates by doing so. Eventually, he turns to the dark side.

Now we have explored the pitfalls of falling in love, is there a resolution? Is there a way to make love between two people sustainably? According to Buddhist monk Thich Nhat Hanh it's possible for a romantically involved couple to experience true love. He argues that true love needs four ingredients: *(1) loving-kindness*, which is the capacity to bring the other person happiness, *(2) compassion*, which is the capacity to have concern for the other person's sufferings, *(3) joy* because it's important to have fun together and not make each other cry all the time and *(4) inclusiveness,* which means that two people become one, and are willing to carry each other's burdens. Hanh's suggestions resemble the Stoic proposition on marriage by Musonius Rufus, who saw mutual care as the key ingredient for a successful union.

> *"In marriage, there must be complete companionship and concern for each other on the part of both husband and wife, in health and in sickness and at all times, because they entered upon the marriage for this reason as well as to produce offspring."*
>
> Musonius Rufus, *Lecture XIII A*

A problem many people face is that they seek relationships while operating from a place of lack, hoping that their partner will fill up their emptiness and make them whole. But such an attitude towards love is risky. If we let our happiness depend on external forces, we put our money on something extremely unreliable. The infatuation phase we experience when we fall in love may make us *feel* complete for a while, but when the so-called honeymoon phase ends, we return to this sense of incompleteness. Hence, after the pink clouds subside, breakups often occur, as people continue seeking that romantic high. But completeness is not something to be found anywhere but in ourselves.

Walking Away

Somehow, many people feel obligated to give away their time and energy to others. But why? Perhaps they feel the need to prove themselves or have an intense desire to be liked? The problem is that by caring too much about the opinions of other people, you become their servant. If you find yourself in that situation often, I will share with you a powerful method to regain your sovereignty and show the world that you value yourself. This method is called: 'walking away'.

Walking away seems rude, but sometimes it's a necessary measure to exert a sense of power over a situation. In a lifetime you meet a variety of people. Some of these people have difficulties respecting other people's boundaries. Some of them are clingy and demand a great chunk of your time. Others are simply cruel assholes that seek to take advantage of people for their own gain. These people deserve to be let go of. When you show these people that you're willing and able to remove yourself from their presence it will not only send them a message that they do not *own* you; it will give *you* back control over your own faculty: your ability to choose and decide for yourself. The power of 'walking away' has two great companions.

1) The word 'no'
2) Direction

If you often find yourself wasting your time on the whims of other people. *Or worse*; you are often being taken advantage of and used or even abused by them, it is very likely that you have difficulties saying 'no' and that you lack direction in life. The inability to say 'no' and the absence of direction in life leads to you not standing firm. If you're not standing firm, you're easily caught up in the affairs of other people.

When people notice that you lack direction - for example in the form of commitment to a personal goal - they will see your time as less valuable than theirs. This observation legitimizes you doing stuff for *them* instead of for yourself. In their eyes, you're at least doing something valuable with your time which is being a utility - for their interest. However, when you *are* committed to a goal, it shows that you value your time and, therefore, your life. People will realize that you're spending your time in ways that are more important than serving *them*.

Also, by keeping your eyes on the ball, it's way easier to walk away from situations in which people violate your boundaries or downright abuse you. This could be the case in regard to the workplace, marriage, and even friendships. Being tethered to your own path results in you caring less about the affairs of others. When you focus on yourself, you will not engage in needy, approval-seeking behavior because there is only one person you have to prove yourself to you.

Walking away from abusive people and destructive environments will protect your self-respect and integrity. It shows the world that you *decide* and are *not decided for*. It shows your friends, family, and spouse that, although you love them, you are not dependent on them and will not stick around when they cross your boundaries. It shows the person you are doing business with that you have plenty of other options and, despite the fact that you're interested, the deal is not a necessity for you.

Walking away creates an abundance mindset. Even if you don't have a lot of money, possessions, or friendships, it signals that you are utterly content. You might *like* and *love* certain people in your life, but you don't *need* them. Luxury, a million dollars in the bank, a Lamborghini; it's all great, but without these external things you'll be perfectly fine as well. The willingness to walk away, and mean it, is your strongest negotiating position, because either way, you win.

Social Minimalism

As explored in previous essays, a minimalist lifestyle concerns itself with minimizing the number of material resources we need to be satisfied. A tremendous benefit of this approach is the reduced cost of living. The less we need, the more time, money, and energy we save. So, can we also apply minimalism to our social connections to gain the same benefits? Can we be happy with a minimal amount of friends, or even without friends?

Ideally, a social minimalist gets by with a minimal amount of social connections: just enough to fulfill his social needs. But many consider living with a few or *without* friends unhealthy and painful. Being friendless deprives us of the benefits of a social group. So, is a lack of friends synonymous with a dreadful existence of loneliness and social isolation? Do the friendless indeed deserve our pity?

People seem to agree that having friends is always better than having none. Therefore, we celebrate the blessing of friends. Having many friendships means we have many options to socialize and, thus, no shortage of pleasurable human interaction. However, as far as the social minimalist is concerned, having *fewer* friends has benefits as well. And, in some cases, going *without* friends is the best option. Can we be happy without friends?

The decline of friendship

The ancient Greek philosopher Epicurus believed that we could attain peace of mind and freedom from suffering by wisely balancing our desires and seeking sustainable, moderate pleasure. He created a hierarchy of needs as a roadmap by dividing *natural and necessary, desires, natural and unnecessary desires*, and *vain desires*. Things like extreme wealth and fame he considered obsolete and impossible to satisfy. But also luxurious food, marriage, and sex, although he thought these desires are *natural*, Epicurus saw them as *unnecessary* for a happy and content existence. But to friendship, he attributed the same value as food and shelter, as he saw it as one of the greatest portals to pleasure and one that's generally easy to obtain.

> *"Of all the means that wisdom acquires to ensure happiness throughout the whole of life, by far the most important is friendship."*
>
> Epicurus, *Sovereign Maxims*

As opposed to romantic love, friendship (also known as 'philia') usually doesn't evoke strong emotions, and there's much less possessiveness and jealousy, and it's more non-committal. Philia centers around shared interests, utility, and enjoying the other person's company.

According to Epicurus, friendship is based on trust, treating each other well, and maintaining a generous attitude. If these criteria are met, friends allow us to share information about the world and our ideas, learn from their experiences, and help them with ours. Friends can lend us a helping hand, a listening ear, and words of advice in times of hardship. Also, being part of a social circle can open doors to various opportunities, like finding a partner. Epicurus chose to live together with friends while enjoying the simple pleasures of eating bread and cheese and drinking weak wine.

If we extrapolate from Epicurus' views, we can see that the benefits of friendship still stand today. Also, we have far more options now, as we can maintain friendships with people in other areas of the world, have friends exclusively online, and communicate with any friend whenever we want. But the emergence of modern means of communication and how today's societies are structured seem to render *traditional* ways of friendship obsolete. Most activities that require a social circle can be obtained elsewhere. For example, we can use services to talk about our problems or to move out. We don't need to leave the house for discourse anymore, as online spaces offer a plethora of online groups, forums, and communities.

Moreover, the likelihood of finding fellow thinkers *online* is much greater than meeting them *offline* because we're not limited to the people in our immediate environment, our cities, or even our countries anymore. And even though online dating was a rarity in the early zeros of the twenty-first century, it has become the norm, meaning that we don't *need* to attend social gatherings anymore to find a mate.

We can also find quick and cheap entertainment through streaming services and video games, which many people *prefer* over a meetup with friends nowadays. So, it appears that the necessity of friendship is slowly eroding and being replaced mainly by the increasing amount of options that technology offers. The coming metaverse will probably accelerate the disappearance of old-fashioned face-to-face interaction, as humanity will largely plug itself into virtual reality.

Some find the idea of a friendless world daunting: how can we possibly live without friends? But traditional friendship also comes with costs and downsides.

The cost of friendship

Having friends is no free ride. Especially today, in our individualistic societies, friendship (in the traditional sense) seems more challenging to obtain than in the times of Epicurus. We focus very much on ourselves, and our busy, hectic lives absorb most of our time and energy. Friends can be a blessing, but they're not essential to survive anymore. As C.S. Lewis stated:

"Friendship is unnecessary, like philosophy, like art, like the universe itself (for God did not need to create). It has no survival value; rather it is one of those things which give value to survival."

C.S. Lewis, *The Four Loves*

For many, an extensive social circle has become a *luxury good*, as friendship seems more challenging to come by these days. It comes with costs that not everyone is willing to make. The first cost we can distinguish is time, which, with our busy lives, is often a scarce commodity. Do we want to exchange the little free time we have for the company of other people? Many choose not to, as they instead spend their free time on solitary activities like creative pursuits. The second cost we can distinguish is energy. We're often so tired during the workweek that we prefer spending our evenings in front of the television. Hence, we commonly practice friendship on the weekends, which means that we spend the energy left after our workweeks on socializing. Therefore, many choose to spend their free time in solitude to recharge.

The third cost would be resources, as socializing requires money in many cases. Having no social life, therefore, *saves* money. But also, the lack of funds *refrains* people from socializing, which *could* cause social isolation among the impoverished. The fourth cost is more hidden but still a price we pay when we engage in social interaction. Friendships require conformity to a certain extent, depending on the people we're dealing with. Consciously or subconsciously, we wish to be liked by our friends and vice versa and meet mutual expectations.

And thus, we present ourselves to appease them and sweep unwanted characteristics under the carpet. So, we pay the price of wearing a mask among our friends, not showing the *entirety* of ourselves, afraid that we fall out of favor. But, as Arthur Schopenhauer stated, we can only truly be ourselves in solitude, in which we can safely cast off our masks as there are no people to consider.

The misery of bad friends

Not all friendships conform to Epicurean ideals. Friendships certainly *can* be a source of misery, especially with those that do not have our best interests at heart. The *Buddha* urged people not to associate with the foolish but with the wise. Associating with bad friends can be harmful and holds us back from associating with the *wise* who can *improve* our lives. If no wise people are available, it's better to walk alone than be accompanied by *bad friends*. One of the earliest Buddhist texts, known as the "Rhino Sutra," advises us to wander alone like rhinoceros.

Avoid the evil companion
disregarding the goal,

intent on the out-of-tune way.
Don't take as a friend
someone heedless and hankering.
Wander alone like a rhinoceros.

Khaggavisāṇa-sutta

Many people have friends just for the sake of having friends. Often, they barely have standards for friendship, so they surround themselves with destructive individuals. For example, we maintain habits like violent behavior and doing drugs to belong to a group that does the same. Or we tolerate and even adopt hateful ideas just to remain connected with those we consider friends. Or we put up with bullying and ridicule by our so-called friends that go beyond playful banter just because we fear not having friends at all. Or we simply just waste our time engaging in meaningless chatter when we have much more productive and pleasurable things to do.

The term 'toxic friend' is widespread these days. Even though we may realize these people are bad for us, we're afraid to let them go because we fear loneliness. So, humans often seem to prefer destructive relationships to solitude, probably because the thought of being alone terrifies many. We depended on the herd for survival for many generations, and social ostracization often meant death—the drawbacks of communal living we had to take for granted. But today, many societies allow us to survive with minimal social contact, which gives us the luxury, to a great extent, of *not* having to associate with people that make us miserable. As Robin Williams famously stated: "I used to think the worst thing in life was to end up all alone. It's not. The worst thing in life is ending up with people who make you *feel* all alone."

Do we need friendship?

Is there a case for social minimalism? Or do we *need* friendships to satisfy our social needs? Psychologist and author Dr. Daniel Marson say that we humans *don't* need to have friends. He acknowledges the vital importance of inter-individual communication for human development. But he also states that, because of this importance, we overemphasize the quality and intensity of social relationships.

> *"We need to interact with each other but it is not necessary that these relationships reach anything more than a basic level of connectedness. It is nice to have strong social relationships but it is not necessary for our survival or even our happiness. Simply put, it is not necessary for humans to have friends."*

Dr. Daniel Marson, *Why You Don't Need Friends*, published in Psychology Today

Marson explains that many people struggle with making and keeping friends and often think very negatively of themselves because of that. So, it's not just the absence of friendship that's the problem, but the notion that there's something wrong with that. According to Marson, a lack of friends is *not* wrong. Not having friends doesn't automatically mean that we're socially isolated and lonely, as there's a gap between "social isolation" and "having friendships." And we can gain the same benefits of friendships simply by the *possibility* to interact with people. So Marson's ideas tell us that a minimalist approach to friendships would be sufficient to satisfy our social needs.

We deem friendship important. But according to a study of about four thousand adults, having our basic needs met and feeling competent in what we do is *more* important. If we compare these outcomes to Epicurus' hierarchy of needs, we can conclude that satisfying our basic needs, our natural and necessary desires, is the cornerstone of our well-being. But, as opposed to what Epicurus believed, friendships may not be so essential.

However, social interaction remains an important, beneficial part of human life. We might want to emphasize the *importance* of social interactions, especially in times when these are forcefully minimized. Also, in our increasingly individualistic cultures, many people *lack* social interaction, even when they *have* friends. Being without friends, in the traditional sense, doesn't seem so problematic. And when we consider the costs and downsides of having friends, it might even be preferable at times. But minimizing social interaction *to the extreme* probably isn't a good idea for most of us. We naturally crave connection with people. It nourishes the spirit. Even if it's just a friendly conversation with the cashier.

Breakups

The philosophy of Taoism revolves around letting go, accepting, yielding, and going with the flow. All Taoist sages seem to agree that it's better to be detached and indifferent, allow change to happen, and move along with life's constant transformations than to *resist* change and cling to what's already in the past. When we are romantically involved with someone, we often see the opposite happening of what the Taoist scriptures advocate. We attach, we cling, we control, and we're usually very fearful of being abandoned by the person who generates immense bliss within us. At the peak of the so-called honeymoon phase,' when everything seems carefree, joyful, and happy, we wish it would never end. But as we all know: this period of mutual infatuation never lasts.

No feeling is final. The changing nature of our emotional world causes us to fall *out* of love, sometimes as quickly as we fall *in* love. When feelings change, the *relationship* changes. Frequently, the consequence of declined feelings of attraction, for whatever reason, is a breakup. Such a drastic change is challenging to handle, especially when the decline in attraction isn't mutual. For some, it takes years (or even a lifetime) to get over someone. Others never truly accept the breakup and move to Heaven and Earth to win back their old flame, to no avail. When we cannot change outside circumstances, the only way to move forward is to change *ourselves*, including how we look at the situation at hand.

Holding on, letting go

The art of letting go is a recurring theme in Taoist texts. In the book of Zhuangzi, we'll find a short story about Pei Kung She, the tax collector. In order to make a set of new bells for the king, he had to collect sufficient taxes. What seemed an impossible task, Pei finished without effort, and within three months, the bells were completed. The king asked: "Master Pei, what is this art you wield?" Then, Pei explained that he didn't wield anything:

> *"Mysteriously, wonderfully, I bid farewell to what goes, I greet what comes; for what comes cannot be denied, and what goes cannot be detained. I follow the rude and violent, trail after the meek and bending, letting each come to its own end. So I can collect taxes from morning to night and meet not the slightest rebuff."*

Zhuangzi, *The Mountain Tree*

Master Pei didn't force anything and got great results. He didn't get into arguments and simply bent with the situations he encountered.

This story has nothing to do so far with breakups. But it displays the Taoist attitude toward life in general,

107

one of going with the flow and letting go of what goes. This attitude is the opposite of how people generally approach romantic love. Instead of letting go, we tend to grasp. And when a breakup occurs, instead of accepting it, we deny what comes and try to detain what goes. But by doing so, we're opposing the way of the universe, so to speak. Not only do we act in opposition to the outside world, but also to ourselves. If we let go, we are soft and supple. If we refuse to let go, we are dry and brittle. From a Taoist point of view, life is soft and supple; death is brittle and dry.

Imagine the hurt caused by the unwillingness to let go of what's already passed. When we keep living in the past, we'll eventually become bitter and unable to allow the present in our lives. Like a river flowing past someone tightly clinging to a rock, life passes by someone refusing to let go of a past relationship. What a waste, as life contains so many opportunities that we cannot see because we've turned our backs on them. When we don't bid farewell to what goes, we seem to be less likely to greet what comes. Because as long as we don't let go of one thing, it's impossible to embrace another.

A blessing in disguise

Once upon a time, the Taoist sage Zhuangzi wandered in the mountains and encountered a vast tree. Its branches were thick and crooked. A lumberjack passed by but refused to cut the crooked tree down. When Zhuangzi asked him why he replied: "There's nothing this tree could be used for! It's worthless!" But Zhuangzi said: "Well, because of its worthlessness, this tree can live out the years Heaven gave it." Again, this Taoist story itself may have nothing to do with heartbreak, but there's a lesson to be learned about the blessing of *rejection*. The woodcutter rejected the tree because it wasn't good enough in his eyes. But this rejection allowed the tree to grow old and beautiful, and over the years, people came to admire it and even declared it a holy place.

Someone rejecting us is just another change that comes with loss but also with gain. Take, for example, the many benefits of being single regarding personal growth, finding meaning in life, and tranquility. And the calmness that's available to us after an emotionally draining relationship ends can be recuperative. We may also come to see that we're not compatible with the person we struggle to let go of, and, perhaps, we're designed for another path that better suits our nature. The crooked tree shows us that not all trees are fit to be turned into wooden planks. Likewise, not all people are suitable for each other. And for some, it may even be better to remain single in certain situations. The crooked tree simply followed its nature; it became what it naturally would become: useless from one perspective but still valuable in the eyes of others.

In accepting the end of a relationship and letting go of someone, we also follow the way fate intends, which is that the person we were once romantically involved with goes another way. As we've learned from the crooked tree: everything has a part to play in this universe. And the roles we've played in the lives of the people we've lost (how unfortunate this may seem) are over.

Embracing impermanence

After letting ourselves become attached to another person, there's often no way to eradicate this attachment overnight. What resists, persists, and the more we fight the pain caused by separation, the more painful it becomes. The attachments that develop between people that are romantically involved are often deep and stubborn. Such a bond either dissolves slowly over time, or it's ripped apart by sudden separation. The latter is painful: the more we attach, the more we grow into each other, and the more drastic the breakup is. When this separation happens, there's a wound that needs time to heal. Many people try to accelerate this process by seeking distractions and repressing thoughts and emotions, but to no avail as the wound heals at a natural pace.

We can choose to keep running from our pain, but we'll have to face it someday, often when we don't expect it. We can choose to fight our pain, but by doing so, it only increases because we put an extra layer of pain on top of the pain that already exists. The more we want to be free of pain, the more pain we experience. So instead of trying to get rid of the pain that comes with letting someone go, we can accept it as an inevitable part of a breakup until it naturally subsides, like cloudiness naturally transforms into a clear sky.

> "*Mastery of the world is achieved by letting things take their natural course. You can not master the world by changing the natural way.*"

Lao Tzu, *Tao Te Ching*, 48

The beauty is that we can trust the universe in solving the problems that we cannot solve ourselves. Even though change seems to work against us when we lose someone we love, it also works to our advantage as it will eventually rid us of our grief and sorrow. And this process itself has valuable things to offer, like becoming familiar with pain which is a root for compassion and empathy. Moreover, the pain of heartbreak has been a source of inspiration for many artists. Impermanence can be a friend or foe, depending on how we treat it. If we continually move in opposition to it, our suffering will be endless. But if we allow it to be, we will enable it to dissolve naturally and we won't suffer the additional pain that comes with resisting what is.

Letting someone go can be a never-ending, painful process if we refuse to move along with the changing nature of the universe. Nothing is permanent. Everything comes and goes, including the people in our lives. Life isn't supposed to play out the way we want, but the way it happens. From a Taoist perspective, nothing that happens is fundamentally wrong or right; it's simply the universe changing. But it's the mind that adds problematic elements to some of these changes, making them undesirable in our eyes. So, we don't suffer change itself, but the way we look at it.

A Taoist sage greets what comes and says farewell to what goes. Change is the natural state of the universe; it moves like the sea's tides, between opposites like ebb and flow, high and low, front and back. If we are supple and flexible towards change, we may start to enjoy the way things are, at the moment, and accept their impermanent nature. A breakup, then, isn't right or wrong, but just another change that we can ride like an ocean's wave.

No Sex

In most modern-day societies, the idea of not having sex may sound preposterous. After all, isn't physical intimacy one of the key ingredients of a healthy and fulfilling life? Well, if that's the case, then we stumble upon a problem, as the visibility of sexuality and eroticism only increases in this age, the frequency of sexual intercourse actually decreases. Recent numbers suggest that people, especially young men, are having less sex than before. So, if we put such a high value on sex and view it as a life necessity, we could say that an increasing number of people are deprived of something essential. But is this truly the case? Do we need sex as much as we think we do? And could *not having sex* even be *beneficial* to us? The purpose of this piece is not to discourage lovemaking or to shame those who do it. It's simply an exploration of reasons *not* to engage in the "pleasure of all pleasures:" sex.

The sacrifice may not be worth it.

In many cases, sex comes with a price. When you're not in a relationship or marriage, obtaining some fun between the sheets can be quite a hassle. And yes, even if you're *with* someone, it can be a rare occurrence. Some say sexless marriages are the rule, not the exception. But let's approach this from the perspective of a single person, who, in order to find a mate, needs to either be physically present at places with potential partners or use online services like dating apps and websites.

First of all, this pursuit will not always be successful. In some cases, dependent on how your target category of people perceives you, it could take a while to find someone who suits your criteria in the physical sense. But even when you manage to find a suitable bed partner, there's always a chance the chemistry is lacking, or there could be performance anxiety. Or worse: the person you just met could turn out to be a dangerous psychopath! Then, of course, there's an option to exchange currency for pleasure. But are you willing to spend your hard-earned money for a moment of carnal fun with a sporting lady or gentleman? Also, one might want to contemplate the conditions and motivations of the people who do this kind of work: they're often pretty unwholesome.

Like with many things in life, the pursuit of intimacy comes with risks. More than two millennia ago, philosopher Epicurus (inventor of a moral philosophy revolving around pleasure) clarified why sexual intercourse was *not* among the pleasures he pursued. The Epicurean stance towards sex is that it's a 'natural desire.' But to be happy and content, which is the ultimate goal of the Epicureans, one does not require the fulfillment of this desire. Moreover, Epicurus argued that sex is *never* beneficial, and you are lucky if it doesn't harm you, implicating that it's harmful by default.

Many would disagree with Epicurus' statement. But research shows a correlation between poor mental health and the frequency of casual sex, also known as ''hookups.' It's not entirely clear if people with poor mental health are more likely to engage in hookups or if hookups cause poor mental health. However, a publication by the *International Academy of Sex Research* suggests that, and I quote:

"Sexual behavior may involve risks to physical and mental health. Physical health consequences include unintended pregnancy, sexually transmitted infections (STIs), and sexual assault."

Fielder, R. L., & Carey, M. P. (2010). Predictors and consequences of sexual "hookups" among college students: A short-term prospective study. Archives of Sexual Behavior, 39(5), 1105-1119.

Whether or not one is willing to accept the potential risks and sacrifices is up to that individual. Perhaps a more straightforward approach to satisfy our carnal desires is articulated by Diogenes. After being asked why he would pleasure himself in public, he replied: "If only it were so easy to soothe hunger by rubbing an empty belly."

The less your scratch, the less it itches

Like all forms of sensual desires, the desire to get one's end away is just another itch that seeks to be scratched. We can either scratch it by engaging in intercourse or by doing it the Diogenesian way. But as long as we keep scratching, the itch remains and might get even worse. Buddhist knowledge of the mind shows us how desires work and how we can get rid of them. To understand this, we must identify the reason *why* we have these desires in the first place. From a Buddhist point of view, engaging in sensuality is a way to escape this nagging feeling of dissatisfaction with life. Even though sensual pleasures are natural and deeply rooted, we could also misuse them to numb pain. And by doing so, they grow stronger.

Addiction is essentially the extreme indulging in sensuality, turning things like eating or surfing the internet into compulsive habits, controlling the addict. The more we scratch, the more we itch. Scratching may temporarily bring relief, but the itch returns more robust and intense after a while. With sex, such mechanisms are at play as well. Many people who'd consider themselves to have a "healthy sex life" could, in reality, be under continuous pressure of their cravings but simply have access to one or more partners that are routinely available as a response *to* their cravings and, thus, a continuation.

Buddhist monk Ajahn Nyanamoli argues that celibacy would be beneficial for a *non*-Buddhist person for the apparent reason that one is *not* controlled by a strong desire that otherwise defines one's whole life.

Being celibate can dry the mind out of the "wetness" of sensual desire, so it becomes free of it.

> *"...because the whole life, a person's life, an average person's life, revolves around following desires and getting what you want, which usually revolves around sensuality, around finding a mate, a family. The whole thing revolves around the very basic desires, that are deeply rooted obviously. So if one is able to go against it in a sense of not just pure denial but in a sense of actually developing wisdom on account of it, like "seeing of desire by not giving in to desire," you can eventually overcome that desire. And then you can imagine the freedom of that mind."*

Ajahn Nyanamoli Thero, *Why Is Celibacy Important*, published on the Hillside Hermitage YouTube channel

From this perspective, the healthiest sex life would be none at all. The less we itch, the less we have to scratch. And according to those who are celibate, not having to scratch *at all* is a huge relief.

A different, more expansive life

Even though giving up sex *seems* like a heavy reduction in life satisfaction, there are numerous personal accounts of celibates that describe experiences of a different yet more expansive life. In an article in the Buddhist magazine *Tricycle*, lay practitioner Mary Talbot describes how celibacy has been one of the most liberating decisions of her life. She writes that eliminating the pursuit of sex and romance freed up tremendous mental space that she previously used to think, analyze, strategy, regret, and agonize.

> *"I was inspired by monks and nuns I know, and by the Buddha's promise that while a celibate life may appear drastically reduced from the outside, the renunciate's inner life blossoms and expands exponentially. My existence as an urban working mother precludes most of what monks and nuns do in the course of a day, but this is a piece of monastic life, along with meditation and seclusion, that I can practice in the privacy of my own home."*

Mary Talbot, *The Joy of No Sex*, published in Tricycle

Removing the pursuit of sex and romances from our lives likely lessens our engagement with the outside world. But this disengagement causes social minimalism which also creates an opportunity for the inner world to blossom. When we look at human behavior, we see that the claim presented by Ajahn Nyanamoli is correct: our lives generally do revolve around the deeply rooted desire for sensuality and finding a mate. Most people build their lives around it, trying to be as attractive as possible to those they yearn for. For a significant part, anticipated sensuality and romance motivate people to look well, for example, by building a muscular physique or using various beauty products and wearing high heels.

Nyanamoli explains that if we choose celibacy, everything that, in some way, facilitates the gratification of our sexual desires loses power over us. Things like the need for social status or bodily attractiveness to attract potential partners become pretty useless, as the removal of the *end* renders its *means* obsolete. This mechanism works in all areas of life. For example, if you don't *require* an expensive house, you don't *need* to earn the necessary income. If you don't *require* status and prestige, you don't *need* to go out of your way to impress people.

By simply not wanting something, we can reclaim vast amounts of energy that we can use elsewhere. For example, The Jesuits, a Christian order, claim that choosing to be chaste and celibate can be a pathway to God. They aim to practice a healthy form of celibacy, not based on repression and denial, but as a *free and conscious choice* fueled by a longing for the divine, so they can *entirely* focus on their relationship with God. But there are non-religious pursuits as well that one can spend their unlocked energy on. And some people even take it a step further.

Alleged 'sexual transmutation.'

Even though he was popular among women, the Serbian-American inventor Nikola Tesla chose to remain celibate throughout his life. Some claim that he was attracted to men. But this belief seems to reflect the failure to understand why a man *wouldn't* be sexually interested in the women that fancy him. In other words: "he must be gay." Even though sexual desire is deeply rooted in us, there *is* more to life than copulation and procreation. Once a womanizer and gambler, Tesla decided to exert self-control over his desires. He was aware of the *impact* that romantic love could have on people (especially inventors) and saw it as a threat to his cause. When asked if he believed in marriage, he answered:

> *"...for an artist, yes; for a musician, yes; for a writer, yes; but for an inventor, no. The first three must gain inspiration from a woman's influence and be led by their love to finer achievement, but an inventor has so intense nature with so much in it of wild, passionate quality, that in giving himself to a woman he might love, he would give everything, and so take everything from his chosen field. I do not think you can name many great inventions that have been made by married men."*

Nikola Tesla

But it wasn't just the absence of diverting elements in his life that contributed to his success; Tesla also claimed that abstinence played an essential role in his creativity. Through his celibacy, he may have entered the field of so-called "sexual transmutation," as he converted his sexual energy into creative energy.

The validity of sexual transmutation is controversial, and its role in Tesla's life remains vague. Even though it's common in Indian religions and Taoism practices, the idea of transmuting one's energy through abstinence lacks scientific proof. Nevertheless, there's a copious amount of *anecdotal* evidence that people benefit from abstaining from sexual release. Among the infamous 'N*Fap' movement, we find many men (and women to a lesser extent) that experience so-called 'superpowers' after a period of abstinence from self-pleasure. Also, legendary boxer Muhammad Ali used to abstain from sex two months before a big fight, as he claimed that this made him unbeatable in the ring. And in 2010, the famous singer Lady Gaga decided to be celibate to protect her creativity.

American philosopher Henry David Thoreau *celebrated* celibacy. In his book Walden, he called chastity the "flowering of man" and described that we could transmute sensuality into purity and devotion. This "generative energy" that usually dissipates by engaging in "the act" can invigorate and inspire us. Genius, Heroism, and Holiness he considered some of the various fruits that chastity brings. So, whether or not sexual transmutation is a myth; it sounds like a valuable benefit and another reason to lay off the action between the sheets.

On the whole, refraining from sex could be a blessing for those who dare to take the step. But looking at human nature, the birds and the bees won't likely disappear from the stage. After all, how can we continue our species without it? Not to speak of how pleasurable it can be. Buddhist monk Ajahn Nyanamoli admits that, despite its benefits, most people will probably *not* engage in celibacy outside of certain religious practices simply because it's "way too hard."

Forgiveness

Feelings of bitterness and revenge are like heavy stones we carry around on our backs. And if we're unable or unwilling to throw these stones onto the ground and walk away from them, we'll not only exhaust ourselves; the load also increases because of new hurtful life experiences. Eventually, we'll carry even more stones until we can't handle the weight anymore and collapse. Resentment hurts. It can eat us up from the inside. Somehow, we believe that the only way to rid ourselves of resentment is when some form of retaliation occurs. But this may never happen. And so, we run the risk of spending the majority of our lives suffering past hurts while our enemies flourish.

As holocaust survivor Viktor Frankl wisely stated: "When we are no longer able to change a situation, we are challenged to change ourselves." We can't change the past, and we can't change others. Our mental well-being doesn't depend on whether or not we get revenge or receive an apology. It depends on how we handle the pain inflicted on us. So, we have a choice. We can choose to stay attached to old hurts and take our suffering to the grave. Or we can choose to take the antidote and let go of our suffering, so we spend the rest of our lives without the heavy burden of resentment. This antidote has a name: *forgiveness.*

First of all, it's probably essential to mention that forgiveness does not equate with forgetfulness. We can forgive someone without forgetting what this person has done. If we'd also *forget* or (perhaps more common) *refuse* to see the reality of a person or situation, we open ourselves up to be hurt again. Therefore, the best option in some cases might be to forgive someone without ever associating with this person again for the sake of self-protection. The Buddha advised not to associate with the foolish, including "fools" with unwholesome intentions.

Accepting that humans are flawed

"Expectations are premeditated resentments," wrote Allen Berger, author of several books about addiction and recovery. Berger pointed out that we often blame other people for our problems, but that in reality, the cause of our suffering doesn't lie with these people, but with our expectations of them. Resentment often stems from expectations not being met and the disappointment this leads to. One of our biggest mistakes is expecting others not to make mistakes; how ironic this may sound. We sometimes put people on a pedestal, projecting all kinds of expectations onto them. For example, we expect a partner always to be caring and interested in what we have to say. Or we expect a friend always to be helpful and willing to listen. But by doing so, we don't see them for the imperfect human beings they are, but as fantasies of them that we've created in our minds.

We often see these fantasies with parents and children. Many parents have high expectations of their children, and vice versa: children expect their parents to be good parents. But these fantasies rarely resemble reality. Stoic philosopher Epictetus commented on the phenomenon of having a "bad" father, saying and I quote:

"Is you naturally entitled, then, to a good father? No, only to a father."

Epictetus, *Enchiridion*, 30

And thus, from a Stoic point of view, not people's behavior causes resentment but our expectations of them. People are inherently flawed. They make mistakes, gossip, betray, lie, and violate our boundaries. Even people we've held in such high regard may end up disappointing us. Accepting this can make it easier for us to let go of our resentment. Why be angry about a reality we can't control?

Contemplating anger and resentment

The Buddha distinguished three basic causes of suffering: *greed*, *ignorance*, and *hatred*. He described hatred as a great stain on the personality because of its destructive nature. We only have to contemplate the terrible things

125

that have happened due to hatred: people getting wounded or killed, bloody wars, and genocide. Hatred is devastating on the inside too. Holding on to resentment is like holding hot coals and waiting for the other to get burned. Despite all the revenge fantasies we conjure in our minds (but never carry out), having a grudge often hurts *us* the most.

We can be mad at the world, at ourselves. We can feel bitter about the unfairness of life or about the things people around us said and did. But no matter how much oil we throw on the flames of our disgruntled minds, we cannot change what happened, nor can we control the universe. We can keep drinking poison, waiting for our enemies to die, but it's *us* who die a painful death in the end. By contemplating the devastating nature of anger and resentment within ourselves and the outside world, we can remind ourselves that it's unwise to let such emotions poise our minds. Therefore, by letting go of these emotions with forgiveness, we stop watering the seeds of destructiveness. It's a win-win situation.

Being mindful of destructive thinking

For some people, forgiveness is as simple as making a decision and moving on. But for most of us, the act of forgiveness doesn't seem so easy. Resentment is stubborn, and despite any resolution we make, negative thoughts and emotions can appear again and take over our mental state. And before we know it, the grudge towards the person we previously forgave is back in full force. Stoic philosopher Seneca was aware of this phenomenon. In his essay *Of Anger*, he noticed that we have a say in controlling our anger, and we should get rid of it when we encounter it. I quote:

> *"A large part of mankind manufactures their own grievances either by entertaining unfounded suspicions or by exaggerating trifles. Anger often comes to us, but we often go to it. It ought never to be sent for: even when it falls in our way it ought to be flung aside."*

Lucius Annaeus Seneca, *Of Anger*, 3-12

The Buddhists are aware of this phenomenon too, and thus stay *mindful* to let go of unwholesome thoughts before they grow and spread like cancer. The latter happens when we hold on to certain memories, fantasies, narratives, or fears about the future. We could see our minds as a garden, and it's *our job* to tend it. We can let bad weeds spoil it, or we can uproot them, throw them out, and prevent new ones from entering. But, to be skillful gardeners, we need to be mindful. The Buddhists propose meditation as *the* method to train the mindfulness muscle. Thus, the decision to forgive is the first step. But the next step is keeping our mental faculties clean by removing and avoiding junk that revokes resentment towards the person we have forgiven. Forgiveness is useless if we can't commit to it.

Not forgetting the positive

Nature has programmed us in such a way that we're more susceptible to negativity than to positivity. This is why many people look in the mirror and mainly see their undesirable aspects. We call this phenomenon the brain's "negativity bias," and it's causing us to see fault rather than merit in those around us. Hara Estroff Marano, editor at large at *Psychology Today*, writes the following on the origins of the negativity bias:

> *"Our capacity to weigh negative input so heavily most likely evolved for a good reason—to keep us out of harm's way. From the dawn of human history, our very survival depended on our skill at dodging danger. The brain developed systems that would make it unavoidable for us not to notice danger and thus, hopefully, respond to it."*

Hara Estroff Marano, *Our Brain's Negative Bias,* Psychology Today

Nature's instruments for survival can be a Godsent until they begin to affect us in destructive ways. Someone's negative characteristics can cloud their favorable traits to such an extent that we cannot see the positive anymore. In our biased minds, this person had begun to embody evil itself. It's pretty difficult not to feel repulsed by someone who doesn't have *any* positive traits - let alone forgive them. But everyone has at least some positive traits. Hence, we might want to look beyond the vast specter of negativity and see that the people we resent are also carrying good within them and that it's human to possess both   evil   and   good.

Choosing love, not hate

There is a tendency among many people to answer hate with hate. But we see that this mostly makes matters worse and often results in violent conflicts and bloodshed. Activist and Baptist minister Martin Luther King Jr. decided to stick to love, as hate, according to him, is too great a burden to bear. He argued that violence is a descending spiral that brings about precisely the thing it seeks to destroy.

> *"Through violence, you may murder the liar, but you cannot murder the lie, nor establish the truth. Through violence, you murder the hater, but you do not murder hate. In fact, violence merely increases hate. Returning violence for violence multiplies violence, adding deeper darkness to a night already devoid of stars. Darkness cannot*

drive out darkness; only light can do that. Hate cannot drive out hate; only love can do that."

Martin Luther King Jr.

Love doesn't necessarily mean that we should engage with people. We can love them from a safe distance, wishing them the best, without getting burned by their flames of malice. Even though the people that hurt us seem resistant to our love and keep giving us poison, choosing "love" over "hate" is still the best option for our *own* mental well-being. Resentment and anger are bad for your health. Resentment is associated with a lower immune system, increased stress, and many physical ailments like heart disease, cancer, and addiction. Anger can result in problems such as high blood pressure, headaches, skin disorders, and abusive behavior. Forgiveness fueled by love melts away our resentment and anger and replaces them with compassion. Compassion is a force that doesn't destroy but empowers; that doesn't hatefully antagonize but calmy recognizes the humanity in every person (despite their flaws). Compassion may not necessarily drive hate out of others, but it definitely drives it out of us and helps us let go of people.

Letting Go of Worry

Worry

The ability to plan for the future is a cornerstone of our civilization. The human race would never have flourished if we didn't organize, arrange, design, prepare, and delay gratification for greater causes. Take, for example, the *Kölner Dom*: a massive cathedral in the German city of Cologne. Its construction began in 1248 and was completed no earlier than 1880, taking into account that the project was halted for about three hundred years. And there are many wonders alike all around the world that required careful planning and dedication, often powered by religious inspiration.

Nevertheless, this meant that generations of people have spent lifetimes building something that they'd never see finished. This phenomenon displays the human how the human capacity for long-term planning can lead to mind-blowing achievements, like traveling to the moon, and, in all likelihood, a manned trip to Mars. But there's a fundamental difference between planning and worrying. Planning is constructive and focuses on our own actions in a conceptual future, while worrying is trying to control the uncontrollable by repeating possible and even unrealistic scenarios over and over again. Our worries can even consist of fantasies that are *totally* out of touch with reality. Therefore, as opposed to planning, it's *destructive*. Nevertheless, we keep worrying because, for some reason, we think that this is going to help us in one way or another. Unfortunately, worrying generally does more harm than good.

The vast majority won't happen

There's one thing certain about the future, which is that the future is uncertain. History has known numerous people that claimed to have the power of foresight, but their predictions have mostly been vaguely true or downright false. And sure, from a deterministic perspective, the future is already written in the stars. But did someone ever succeed at reading them?

As long as we're constrained by time, we perceive the future as an empty canvas. Anything can happen, which is a *blessing* and a *curse* at the same time. Our minds, however, do not like uncertainty. This is why religions that offer answers regarding human destiny can be so comforting, as they feel secure because they fill the empty canvas with something substantial. But even for a religious person, life can be extremely daunting: as they might have knowledge about the afterlife; *whether* they'll be sent to heaven or hell, or what life on earth has in store for them is still a mystery.

Faced with an uncertain future, our minds tend to create possible scenarios. When it comes to preparedness, this is actually a good thing. Because thinking ahead gives us an advantage, as we calculate the possibilities, we can take the necessary measures based on speculations. For example, knowing that financially difficult times are coming, we can prepare for them by spending less and saving more.

But when we worry, our minds are mass-producing predictions, even about things that don't really matter, and, even worse, repeating them over and over again. The problem is that in the present moment, a situation in which we have created hundreds of possible outcomes unfolds only in one particular way. Moreover, chances are that this situation won't even happen! We could figure out a million possibilities and still be wrong. What's the point of the impossible task of figuring out *exactly* what the future is going to bring? There's no point. As author Eckhart Tolle states: "worry pretends to be necessary but serves no useful purpose".

We can't control the future

Trouble arises when we try to control the future. To control the future, the mind tries to think about it as if it were the present. The mind somehow thinks that by calculating every possible option, it will gain control in the end. If we'd know what exactly would happen, then we'd indeed have an advantage in regard to our own actions: we'd know, for example, when our relationships end, and what stocks we need to buy to become rich. But the future is still out of control; the only difference is that we already know what happens, which makes it no different than the past. We can't control the past, either. The only thing we can control is our own actions in the here and now.

A cause for procrastination, for example, is the inability to retreat from the past and future and focus on the task at hand instead. In the present moment, we can create a new past, and influence the future, but this requires us to keep our focus on what we can do right now. By compartmentalizing a task, we can work on manageable pieces, which makes it much easier to focus, as we forget the end result for a while, and only think in terms of hours, sessions, or days. This relieves us from the undermining weight of goals that seem almost impossible to reach, while still working on them in the best possible ways.

Worrying only keeps us from acting. And the more we live in the future, the more our anxiety sabotages our efforts to make a change. As it's written in the Bible: *"Therefore do not worry about tomorrow, for tomorrow will worry about itself. Each day has enough trouble of its own."*

We often don't value certain events properly

A hallmark of chronic worriers is that they desire certain outcomes while being averse to others. For example, many people worry about social interaction because they want to be liked, or they worry about their jobs because they're terrified of losing them. By exploring many possible scenarios, the mind tries to *prevent* what it's averse to from happening and *incur* what it desires. But, again, the future is uncertain. And for that exact reason, we don't know if the things that we want to happen are truly good, and things that we *don't* want to happen are truly bad.

There's a Taoist story that portrays what happens to people who judge based on what they don't know. This story tells about an old farmer, whose horse ran away. After they heard the news, his neighbors came to visit and said:

"Such bad luck."
"Maybe," answered the farmer.

But the next morning the horse came back, accompanied by three *wild* horses.

"That's so wonderful," the neighbors exclaimed.
"Maybe," replied the old man.

The next day, the farmer's son tried to ride one of the wild horses, but he was thrown and broke his leg.

"What a misfortune," the neighbors said full of sympathy.
"Maybe," answered the farmer.

The next day, military officials came to the village to draft the farmer's son into the army. But when they noticed the broken leg, they passed him by. Then, the neighbors congratulated the old farmer, telling him how lucky he is that his son is spared from war.

The farmer replied: *"maybe."*

This Taoist story shows that we can't judge what's desirable or undesirable when it comes to present events, because we don't know how things will turn out. Things that seem bad, may turn out to be blessings (and vice versa). So, there's no point in desiring certain outcomes if we cannot judge their value. Maybe losing a job is the best thing that could happen to us. Maybe losing our money leads to us living a much happier life. We just don't know. But it's comforting to keep in mind that every cloud has a silver lining.

To conclude this piece, it's essential to mention that worrying is terrible for our health according to copious amounts of research. Worrying comes from a place of fear, and only generates more fear, which makes it a vicious downward spiral. The chronic anxiety that comes from worrying affects the immune system and can lead to physical illness. When we become more receptive to illness, we have given ourselves yet another thing to worry about. Being aware of the devastating consequences, combined with the knowledge that the majority of the things we worry about won't happen, and that we can't correctly judge future events, we might want to prioritize our mental hygiene over all those things that we can't control anyway.

Nostalgia

People are divided about how we should approach these intense experiences related to past events, called *nostalgia*. We all have different relationships with the past. Some people just love to immerse themselves in memories, others avoid them like the plague. Some have made peace with their past, others are haunted by it. Most people have at least a couple of pleasant past memories of times when life was good.

Recollecting these past events can, therefore, be pretty enjoyable to some; especially if these events concern shared memories enjoyed in the company of those whom we share them with. But to others, thinking about those good old times evokes sadness. We might long for those past events, wishing they'd return while simultaneously realizing that our current situation is not so pleasant. Unfortunately, what's done is done: the old time won't come back. Yet, many people are stuck in the past.

After King Nebuchadnezzar II successfully besieged Jerusalem in 597 BC, the inhabitants of the Kingdom of Judah were deported to Babylon. In the book of Psalms, we can find an expression of yearning by the Jewish people.

"By the rivers of Babylon, there we sat down, yea, we wept, when we remembered Zion."

This Jewish hymn, also known as "by the rivers of Babylon" is an example of the human phenomenon of grieving intensely about the past. Sometimes these grievances are just temporary and in other cases, we see people in an almost perpetual sadness grown from a deep longing for what's already gone. For the Jewish people in exile, this didn't mean that the city of Jerusalem was gone; the city is still here today. They mourned their former presence in Jerusalem.

Nostalgia concerns our personal relation to the environment. For those in exile, many memories were created in the city of Jerusalem; things like youth, friendships, childbirth, or good times with family members. Therefore, the Jewish people had become attached to this city. In their collective story, Jerusalem is *their* city. But their deportation by the enemy meant an involuntary abandonment of the place they were so attached to together with both individual and collective stories related to it.

Jerusalem had become part of their identity. By leaving it behind, they got separated from themselves; how strange this may sound. Nevertheless, the Jewish people started a new phase in their lives. When we enter a new phase in our lives, our brains tend to romanticize the phases before. We hear, see or smell something that reminds us of those times in the past - like a song, a photo, or perfume, and we feel these weird sensations in our stomach or suddenly find ourselves in a full-blown emotional ensemble. The weird thing I've noticed about nostalgia is that we are nostalgic about times we were nostalgic about earlier times. When I was twenty years old, I was nostalgic about the times I was twelve. When I was twenty-seven, I was nostalgic about the times I was twenty, when I was thirty-two, I was nostalgic about the times I was twenty-seven, and so forth.

When we look at it, it doesn't make any sense to long for a period of time and, a few years later, long for the period of time in which you were longing for another period of time. The Jewish people were in agony when they were deported, but it won't surprise me that some of them looked back on that time of deportation with nostalgic feelings afterward. War, for example, is considered a terrible thing. How come, people who experienced the second world war, can be quite nostalgic about it sometimes? There are many stories about solidarity and heroism in wartime; things we barely experience when times are peaceful.

A more contemporary example is quitting a job. When we quit a job, we hate we are full of joy. But after a year or so we may long back for the pointless conversations at the coffee machine and the stupid jokes from certain coworkers. Our time working there has become nostalgic, and we tend to think; "oh, now I realize how great that job actually was. I wouldn't mind working there again." But do we base this statement on facts? Or do we base it on emotions evoked by mere memories?

The word *nostalgia* is composed of the Greek words; *nostos* and *algos*. The word *nostos* refers to *returning home*. The word *algos* refers to sorrows and grief. According to *Oxford Languages*, nostalgia is a sentimental longing or wistful affection for a period in the past. Therefore, the experience of nostalgia is based on memories: things remembered from the past.

The problem with memories is that they aren't the same as reality. They're very subjective constructions of events that are behind us; fantasies about a realm outside of the present moment, that are so beautifully engraved in our minds. Relationships may be the finest example of this. Why do so many people crave back their exes even though the relationship or marriage was highly dysfunctional? When a physically abusing, alcoholic spouse dies because of, let's say, cancer, years later, the one left behind tends to look back on the marriage and think: "It's only now that I realize how beautiful our marriage actually was." So, we could ironically conclude that the spouse's death was a blessing for the marriage. As said in the previous chapter, people don't know how to let go which leads to worrying.

Appealing to collective nostalgia is an effective political strategy. Many people long for how the country was in the past and wish that those times would come back. So, they fall for the promises of a politician to revive those old times. However, the only thing that we can recreate similar circumstances, but in no way, we can bring back the past. The Buddha recommended not to dwell in the past or desire it:

> *"The past should not be followed longing after and the future neither desired nor urged for! What is past, not real anymore, is dead & gone, and the future, not real now, has yet to come!"*

Gautama Buddha, *Majjhima Nikaya III*, 131

There is nothing wrong with bringing up past memories sometimes, and in some cases, it's even necessary to reflect in order to plan for the future. But clinging to the past is just another form of suffering. We either let past negative experiences hurt us over and over again, or we desire moments that simply aren't there anymore and will not return unless we find a way to travel back in time. I'd like to add that the nature of our memories makes the past unreliable as well, simply because they are a recreation by the mind and, thus, *not* the real thing. *"We suffer more often in imagination than in reality,"* Seneca once stated.

Being caught up in our imagination means that we are avoiding the present moment. Nostalgia comes from dissatisfaction with the present moment and hinders us from appreciating the period we're living in, only when it's gone do we remember its beauty of it. But by clinging to things not really there, we don't just escape the present;

we also resist the changing nature of our existence. When we realize that the moments we desire are gone we experience sadness. "Get busy living or you get busy dying," is a famous quote from *The Shawshank Redemption*. When we refuse to live in the present despite the ever-changing nature of the universe, we suffer. Yet, many people spend great amounts of their lives residing in fantasies about times that are gone. Therefore, nostalgia is not only a clinging to the past, but a human rebellion against impermanence as well.

What We Don't Know

mystery

noun

Something strange or not known that has not yet been explained or understood.

There's this human tendency to find explanations for things we don't understand. This tendency has been the birthplace of folklore and creation stories that are the cornerstones of many religions. Imagine living in the tribal age, gazing at the stars on a clear night, illuminated by the light of a full moon. How mysterious the world must be, without the knowledge of celestial bodies that we have now. How unexplainable life must be, without any understanding of evolution. The quest for answers has propelled us into exploration, science, and technological advancements that have dragged prehistoric humans from caves into offices. We know more about the environment and the history of terrestrial life than ever before. And with a manned mission to a neighboring planet in the near future, we are ready to enter new territory.

But despite a vast and growing understanding of the cosmos, many things are still uncertain; things as the existence and nature of God and the secrets that hide in the endless blackness that surrounds us. Who are we? Who started this? Was it God? And if yes, what does God look like and why were we put here? Or do we, perhaps, live in a simulation? Like many things that we simply don't know, questions like these irritate people, as human beings tend to be restless in the face of chaos.

For some reason, we *must* have answers, and if we don't, we're willing to construct them ourselves, often based on very simplistic, incomplete ideas, or even downright nonsense. Thus we're willing to commit philosophical suicide, just to get one more riddle out of the way. There are even wars fought, in which people die to defend their ideas, which makes it seem that, for humans, a light in the darkness of mystery is worth dying for.

Humans are on an ongoing crusade for truth, a holy war against the unknown, in pursuit of unraveling the mysteries of life. Unfortunately for us, the mystery will always prevail, and any attempt to understand everything will leave us confused. But what if we are okay with mystery? What if we accept, and even appreciate, that for the most part, existence will remain a mystery to us? What if we *trust* the unknown instead of fearing it? This video explores the beauty of what we just don't know.

The nature of mystery

The human pursuit of creating understanding out of the unknown takes place on many levels. Existentially, for example, humankind, across all cultures and continents, has always concerned itself with the origins of our species and the meaning of life.

One of the oldest creation myths that we know is called *The Eridu Genesis*, created by the Sumerians. *Sumer* was an ancient civilization in the region between the Euphrates and the Tigris. The surviving portion of the tablet on which their creation myth was written, tells the story of how the gods An, Enlil, Enki, and Ninhursanga created their people. It also tells about a flood that the gods sent to destroy mankind, and how the god Enki warned the Sumerian king Ziusudra to build a large boat. We see many similarities between these stories across different cultures and an overall trend to use symbols and archetypes to make sense out of mystery and ease the wound of 'not knowing.'

Mystery manifests itself in many ways. Take, for example, the riddles of the past and future. Even though what's happened in the past cannot be changed, we'll always be guessing what happened *exactly*. First of all, it's because our experience of past events is limited. We've only observed it through our own senses. Sure, we can complement our own stories with the experiences of other people, but *their* experiences are limited as well, and won't recreate the past as it truly was. Moreover, people's memories tend to be distorted, subjective, and erode when time passes. The past, at least how we perceive it in the present, is flawed. It's a collection of memories and

147

recordings that might be extensive but are always subject to the mystery of what we didn't catch on to.

The future is even more mysterious, as we simply don't know what's going to happen next. Looking at the human fixation on prognoses and projections, especially in areas like the stock market, it seems that we're obsessed with clarifying the unknown of what lies ahead. We're even willing to spend money on people who claim to have the ability of foresight. We also love the ideas of prophetic dreams, hunches, and destiny; believing that we have at least *some* control, *some* certainty, and *some* insight about the time to come.

Many predictions are based on the present, which is the most reliable source of knowledge, as we're living in it right now. However, there's no way, at least not for a human, to comprehend everything that happens at this moment. For every answer, thousands of new questions arise, and before we know it we've fallen into the trap of analysis paralysis.

Therefore, the present, even though it's accessible, is still utterly elusive. We don't know what other people think, we don't know what's happening lightyears from here, we don't know what lies beyond the visible universe, and what exactly keeps all of this going. Thus it's understandable that devoid of ultimate knowledge, people are very industrious when it comes to making life (as well as death) as *certain* as possible, so it becomes more bearable. Uncertainty leads to worries and this human will for certainty, however, creates problems.

The human desire for understanding

In the same way, people fight for land and resources, they fight for the truth. This isn't strange, because, with chaos all around us, there's a huge demand for clarity. Those who have the truth, have power, as people follow the ones that can provide them relief from uncertainty. Many of these ideas that supposedly explain the unknown are turned sacred: they become *unquestionable*. This is the definition of dogma.

The phenomenon of dogma is not limited to religion; we can also see this with die-hard atheists, or people that strongly believe in conspiracy theories. And it's also to be found in science. This approach to reality can lead to conflict. It's *our* truth versus *their* truth, like dogs fighting over an invisible bone.

For ourselves, the attachment to certain beliefs can be very limiting. So, just to ease the pain that comes from the inability to deal with meaninglessness and ambiguity, people adopt explanations, from simple theories to complete belief systems. Convinced of their ideologies they walk the earth with certainty, as they *know* the truth. But no matter what truth we adopt, there always seems to be evidence that the ideas we embrace aren't foolproof. This means that we must remain steadfast in

149

our convictions even when the world around us proves us wrong. Such an attitude makes us *rigid*; closed off from what's truly going on as well as new experiences.

On the other hand, if we try to understand too much, we might get stuck in the act of accumulating knowledge. As opposed to the dogmatic individual, the uncertainty combined with a persistent dissatisfaction with possible answers keeps us from making a move. We've become *unwilling* to face chaos without complete knowledge of it; something that's unattainable, yet necessary if we wish for certainty.

The value of faith and trust

So, what if we decide to stop pushing this Sisyphean rock uphill? What if we cease to try to understand it all, to predict what's going to happen, to answer all questions simply to shield ourselves from this terrifying abyss of the unknown? How can we be okay with 'not knowing', and, thus, navigate through life confidently without needing an intellectual safety net?

Well, there's something to be said about the way religious people approach uncertainty. Even though many solve philosophical problems with a belief system, they've at least developed this ability called *faith*. The beauty of faith is the acknowledgment that reason and logic can only bring us so far. By having faith, we accept that beyond the frontiers of our understanding, we simply don't know. And that despite the mystery of it all, we start walking, boldly, knowing that everything is possible.

True faith, in my opinion, means that we stop asking questions, and just make a move toward the darkness, holding the torch of complete trust. Instead of staring anxiously into the abyss, we roll the hard six, and jump right into it. We decide to be okay with mystery, and thus, we make an agreement with the unknown, which is what trust fundamentally is. We stop hiding from it, we stop doubting. We confront it with our heads held high; open to whatever it reveals to us. This way we free ourselves from an endless, vain, depressing pursuit, and enjoy the beauty of what we just don't know.

Letting Go

This piece is not intended to invalidate the importance of control. In some cases, control - especially self-control - is necessary. We need it to plan, work, and engage in relationships. But too much of it is counterproductive and a waste of energy. In many cases, instead of exerting control, it might be a better idea to *let go*. Moreover, letting go at the right moment will lead to much more satisfaction and better results.

Control freaks. We all know them. They think that by pulling all the strings in their environment they will, somehow, improve it, or at least, make it bearable. But their very string-pulling is making their lives unbearable in the first place. And not only *their* lives; the lives of *others* as well. The core motivator for controlling freaks is fear. They fear that when they do not pull the strings, everything will fall apart. Well, probably *some* things will fall apart when they stop controlling them. But, most likely, it won't be the catastrophe that they fear.

Control freaks cannot bear being out of control and surrendering to the moment just isn't an option. I think it's understandable that people do not value the power of letting go, as letting go is often seen as a form of passivity. Especially in this age of prestige and achievement, passivity is looked down upon. Some people are so afraid of being passive that they rather just do something, even when this makes a situation worse, than just let it be, knowing that this is probably the best option. Because when you're doing *something*, people at least perceive you as useful and you might experience a sense of control. While, when letting things run their course, people might see you as passive, uninterested, or even weak.

The power of letting go is hidden in a paradox. To discover this power, we need to understand how the paradox works. This is where a sage named *Lao Tzu* comes in. Lao Tzu is the author of the most important scripture in Taoism, called the *Tao Te Ching*. This book is a short manual for life, that contains an overlooked philosophy also known as 'Wu Wei'. Wu Wei can be translated as effortless action or, simply, non-action.

One who seeks knowledge
Learns something new every day.
One who seeks the Tao
unlearns something new every day.
Less and less remains
until you arrive at non-action.

When you arrive at non-action,
nothing will be left undone.
Mastery of the world is achieved
by letting things take their natural course.
You cannot master the world
by changing the natural way.

If we'd put the idea of letting go into practice, we'll notice a few things. First of all, we discover that many problems often solve themselves; they do not need our intervention. Moreover, by intervening we may make things worse. Aside from the things we *do* control, which is, in a nutshell, our own actions, everything lies in the hands of a universe that is completely out of control.

We can also apply the idea of letting go of situations in which people say nasty things about us: this is not in our control. So, why not let it go? Time heals all wounds. And by taking a step back and just observing, we create a space for nature to let things play out as they will. The anger we might have dissolved, and people's opinions change all the time.

The power of letting go applies to very simple and mundane things, like cooking a meal or flying an airplane. A great part of these activities involves non-intervention. Another example is a *wound* on the body; it's often difficult not to touch it, but only if we keep our hands off it'll heal naturally. Also internal wounds, like grief over a breakup, often heal quickly by just sitting with it and letting it erode.

Who can be still until their mud settles
and the water is cleared by itself?
Can you remain tranquil

until the right action occurs by itself?
The Master doesn't seek fulfillment.
For only those who are not
full are able to be used which
brings the feeling of completeness.

Lao Tzu, *Tao Te Ching*, 15

When we let go, we abstain from grasping. This doesn't mean that we should never grasp but, in many cases, it is unnecessary if we seek a sense of fulfillment and completeness. Not only does the universe take care of itself; the very act of clinging often has a detrimental effect.

It's not a surprise that people generally do not like controlling freaks. Control freaks often experience problems with interpersonal relationships, because the people around them feel controlled. And in the workplace, more often than not, a control freak is destructive to the overall performance of the team. This might be why Lao Tzu wrote that the best leaders are the ones that are not overly controlling:

The best leaders are those
the people hardly know to exist.
The next best is a leader who is loved and praised.
Next comes the one who is feared.
The worst one is the leader that is despised.

According to Lao Tzu, trust is key. If we don't trust people, they will become untrustworthy. And we can only let go, sit back, and relax, if we trust the universe enough to become receptive to what it throws at us in a particular situation, knowing that we will cope. Trust also plays a part in any activity we engage in, from writing to sports. By letting go of our mental blocks and just *doing it*, we *become* the activity. We experience this when we are completely immersed in something, which is also known as the flow state. In this flow state, it's almost like the poem writes itself, the song sings itself, and the dance dances itself. There is no separation anymore between us and the action. The action takes no effort, as it goes naturally and without the intervention of thought. In my opinion, this is one of the most profound examples of *letting go*.

By letting go, we create space for the universe to do its thing. The workings of nature will not cost us any additional energy. And if we are really able to tap into this force, we can get a free and effortless ride, like a sailor riding the waves.

FOMO

Desire can be a significant hindrance to living a purposeful and tranquil life. As soon as we want something, we fall into a state of lack and feel restless. And the obvious way out is to fulfill that desire so that we can feel content and happy again. A much-discussed phenomenon in the current age that arouses such restlessness and lack is the so-called fear of missing out, also abridged as FOMO.

The fear of missing out occurs in many different scenarios. For example, a stock market investor fears that he'll miss out on profits when he doesn't invest in a specific stock at a particular moment. Another example is a college student who never misses a party because she fears that she'll miss out on the fun.

FOMO often drives people mad. Studies show that the fear of missing out can lead to extreme dissatisfaction and can be hazardous to our mental and physical health. FOMO is associated with loneliness, depression, and anxiety. Thus, behind this trendy acronym hides a dark, devastating experience amplified through social media, which presents a never-ending tsunami of snapshots of our lives' highlights. But where does this fear come from? What do people who suffer from FOMO actually fear? And how can we shut it down?

The futility of not wanting to miss out

If we look closely at the fear of missing out, we might ask ourselves the following question: *are we afraid to miss out on what we think we miss out on? Or, are we afraid to experience the pain of having missed out?* It seems that the very occurrence of having missed out on something lies at the center of FOMO, and not so much the thing we miss out on itself.

Take, for example, the student who knows it's better not to go to that party on the college campus because she's broke and needs to study that weekend. Eventually, she decides to go nonetheless. And the reason is not the party itself, as it's just a dime in a dozen; it's the frightening idea of having missed out on something (anything!) that others have not. Or: that she wasn't part of the *story* she shares with others, with those who also have that experience, and not being the odd one out by not having experienced it and being judged because of that.

But what if there weren't any parties at all, perhaps due to a contagious virus? Would she then experience the fear of missing out as well? Probably not, because when there are no parties, *no one* attends parties, so there's nothing to miss out on that others wouldn't miss out on. Thus, there's an element of comparison that seems to play a crucial part in "the fear of missing out," which is that "I fear that I might not have what others *do* have. But if others *don't* have it, then it's okay for me not to have it either."

We can see this element of comparison with investors in, for example, the stock market or the more speculative and volatile crypto market. Again we could ask ourselves what the dominant aspect of their fear of missing out is. Is it just the fear of missing out on profits? Or is the fear of the painful experience of seeing everyone else making profits while you aren't?

"Comparison is the thief of joy," American president Theodore Roosevelt once stated. The fear of missing out seems especially built on a sense of comparison; not having what others have, not being able to experience what others experience. But living life keeping up with the rest of the world is like carrying water to the sea.

In reality, we miss out all the time. Modern life offers us so many choices, and there are so many things happening on this globe, that we humans, with our short life spans, miss out on almost *everything*. We can't have it all. But in an age in which we don't just have an abundance of options, but these options are also unprecedentedly visible to us through the media, we're even more cursed with the awareness that we'll only ever have and experience a fraction of what's out there.

The more we desire to have everything, the more we feel we have nothing. If we don't cease to want it all, we cannot be content, and there will always be something we fear missing out on. Instead, we might want to change our perspective regarding what we *need* and how important the things we desire truly are.

Counting your blessings

Human beings tend to focus on what they don't have rather than on what they do have. In the case of FOMO, the pain of missing out is more significant than the joy of the many things we've not missed out on. Isn't this human discontent an ingenious setup by nature? The dissatisfaction with what we have, and the appetite to get more, have been essential ingredients of our success as a species. But these internal drives can also have negative side effects: restlessness, displeasure, unhappiness, envy, and, yes, a fear of missing out.

The ancient Greek philosopher Epicurus made clear that our desire for more goes at the expense of enjoying what we have:

> *"Do not spoil what you have by desiring what you have not; remember that what you now have was once among the things you only hoped for."*

Epicurus, *Letters (Bobbs-Merrill, 1964)*, XXXV, p. 68

A simple way to release ourselves from this desire is to shift our focus. Instead of concentrating on what we *don't have*, we can look at what we *do have*. To make it

160

practical: we can start counting our blessings by making a list of things we're grateful for. We can contemplate something we haven't missed out on that outweighs the thing we fear to pass by. Sure, we might miss out on that very thing, but how terrible is that, considering what we already have experienced and accomplished? If we've been to ten college campus parties in a row, is it vital to attend the eleventh as well? If we made some decent profits in the past on stocks, is it a disaster if we miss the boat once or twice?

Looking at it from a different perspective

Often, in the ever-fleeting present, some event or opportunity may appear as something huge to us. But when we look back at it, we notice that its gravity decreases over time. How many of the things we deemed so necessary five years ago have lost their significance? And how much will it matter ten years from now if we miss out on what we currently fear to miss out on? We, humans, are inclined to attach ourselves to things in the present that are *insignificant* if we look at them from a broader perspective.

The Stoic emperor Marcus Aurelius reminded himself repeatedly of the world's impermanence and how we're often concerned with stuff that eventually turns into smoke and dust anyway. He encourages us to watch ourselves from a different angle so we realize how insignificant we are:

"To see them from above: the thousands of animal herds, the rituals, the voyages on calm or stormy seas, the different ways we come into the world, share it with one another, and leave it. Consider the lives led once by others, long ago, the lives to be led by others after you, the lives led even now, in foreign lands. How many people don't even know your name? How many will soon have forgotten it?"

Marcus Aurelius, *Meditations*, 9-30

By looking at the world from a cosmic point of view we can put the things we fear to miss out on in perspective. Again, attending an upcoming party may seem like the most important, meaningful thing in the world today. But ten years from now, we have likely forgotten that it ever even happened. And if that's the case, not approaching this event in a matter of days or weeks but in a matter of years or even centuries renders it pretty frivolous. We, then, could ask ourselves: what will we truly miss?

Knowing what you're getting yourself into

Lastly, the things we deem desirable may not be as great as we imagine them. Many of us base our future projections on (idealized) past experiences. But when we finally experience what we anticipated, chances are it disappoints us and brings about negative consequences that we had overlooked or forgotten. When FOMO dominates our decision-making, we've clouded our judgment about the thing we fear to miss out on. Just because everyone wants it doesn't mean it's a good idea. People are herd animals, which sometimes leads to us collectively chasing something that we typically consider undesirable. With enough peer pressure, we even begin to fear that we miss out on things like violence and war.

We pay the ultimate price for attending an overcrowded party, save up money a whole year just to queue up at an understaffed airport, sit in an airplane like sardines in a can, to finally lay down on a cram-full beach. Hence, we travel the world compulsively as if we're attending an all-you-can-eat buffet, just to flood our social media accounts with pictures showing off our extraordinary lives, but then to be disappointed by the lack of 'likes' we receive. Hence, we tolerate horrible hangovers again and again, in exchange for a few hours of pleasure the night before, and are exhausting ourselves by engaging in pointless conversations and faking smiles at dinner parties with people we don't even like. Why? Well, probably, for a major part, because we want to belong.

But the need to belong comes with a price. And the more this need controls us, the more inauthentically we live our lives, and the more we waste our time on things we don't like. Or even worse: we do things that are *bad* for us. Take, for example, people with a drinking problem. Problem drinkers know that it's better to pass up the alcohol, but the fear of missing out, among other things, keeps their destructive habit intact. All those fun evenings at the pub, those drunk Saturday nights at the nightclub, who wants to miss that? But if they would contemplate the long-term consequences of their behavior in detail, then they might conclude that these far outweigh the pleasure drinking brings.

An effective way to shut down FOMO would be to contemplate the negative aspects of the things we fear to miss, creating a realistic image of what we get. We could use a variation of the modern Stoic "praemeditatio malorum," also known as the "negative visualization," for this. Modern Stoics use this exercise to visualize the possible negative events that could happen during the day, so they'll be well prepared for them and, thus, won't be surprised by an unpleasant fate. When we're struggling with FOMO, we could likewise list the negative aspects of the thing we fear to miss out on. The difference is, of course, that we don't walk out the door and engage with it anyway but wisely avoid it. And once we realize that we've made a good choice for ourselves in the long run, we feel better as "missing out" isn't a tragedy but a victory.

The approach by Stoic philosopher Epictetus may be the most appropriate when it comes to keeping ourselves from indulging in mindless pleasures. I quote:

"If you are struck by the appearance of any promised pleasure, guard yourself against being hurried away by it; but let the affair wait for your leisure, and procure yourself some delay. Then bring to your mind both points of time: that in which you will enjoy the pleasure, and that in which you will repent and reproach yourself after you have enjoyed it; and set before you, in opposition to these, how you will be glad and applaud yourself if you abstain.

And even though it should appear to you a seasonable gratification, take heed that its enticing, and agreeable and attractive force may not subdue you; but set in opposition to this how much better it is to be conscious of having gained so great a victory."

Epictetus, *Enchiridion*, 34

The News

We all know that listening to news channels put pressure on our nerves. As soon as we turn on the radio or television or scroll through our social media feeds, a rush of tragic events scourges our minds. From pandemics to street violence, from clashes between countries to changes in climate: if we immerse ourselves in these messages long enough, the world becomes a terrible place.

It's not that the events portrayed by the news are, as a rule, unimportant. Or that we should deny the fact that terrible things happen. Also, in some cases, the media provide us with helpful information and can motivate us to engage in actions that benefit ourselves and others. But, overall, being exposed to the media might do more harm than good. A growing body of research indicates that repeated negative news makes us feel unsafe. Misinformation and fake news can lead to unnecessary chaos, panic, and fear. Unfortunately, the amount of doom available for us to inject into our minds is unprecedented, and how we've gotten used to absorbing lots of information from many different sources.

When it's all doom and gloom out there, one's view of the outside world tends to be bleak. But is the world as terrible as news sources paint it to be?

Information is profit

When dealing with this unending stream of information, it's essential to remind ourselves that the media are generally companies motivated by profit. In short, the media sells information in exchange for our attention, which makes them money. For the most part, this seems like a fair deal. However, what we point our attention to may greatly influence how we think and feel, forming our perceptions. If we predominantly expose ourselves to hateful messages, then our attitude most likely becomes hateful. Nazi politician Joseph Goebbels, for example, knew about the power of propaganda and successfully used it to indoctrinate the German people.

So, for the common good, one would expect the media to deliver information carefully and responsibly. But this rarely seems to be the case. Sure, there are different flavors of media; some tend to be more independent, objective, and well-researched. Others tend to be more about spectacle. Some lean more towards religion; others represent a particular political flavor. But, by and large, it's a competitive business that pursues ratings (and, thus, profit) over charity. Hence, their information should *sell*. Things like conflict, controversial topics, catastrophes, and violence attract people's attention. Companies but also individual content creators know this and often try to capitalize on such issues. They add catchy titles and entertainingly present them: not because it's a correct representation of reality, but because it sells.

Ultra-selective perception of reality

During the last centuries, especially the last decades, the media have radically changed. We went from newspapers and rumors spread from mouth-to-mouth to live streaming on social media from all parts of the world. But there's one thing that news outlets of all ages have in common, namely, their selective nature. News, whether you receive it from a street vendor in Amsterdam in the nineteenth century or from a large news company today: it's always an ultra-selective perception of reality. Many events that people may deem newsworthy never reach the news. Furthermore, the vast majority of things that happen on this planet people don't consider newsworthy in any way. An older woman feeding her cat, a car driving on the highway, a pinecone falling from a tree; these are changes, events taking place, just like what we see in the news. Yet, are they in any way less significant? It's just a matter of opinion. But the fraction of reality that *makes* the news gets amplified and thus made more prominent than it initially appears.

The rabbit hole

The internet has made it possible for everyone to distribute news. Aside from large news companies, there's an increasing number of smaller and individual creators that people choose as information supplies. An advantage of this decentralized way of information distribution is the variety of news sources and access to what's going on at a grassroots level. But there's also a disadvantage. Today, anyone can talk about anything; there's little quality control and a lot of misinformation.

We also see the emergence of echo chambers that revolve around certain topics and beliefs. And these topics may be controversial, and beliefs biased or downright false. Also, the algorithms of several popular platforms recommend content that matches previously watched content. As a consequence, the user quickly tumbles down deeper and deeper into a rabbit hole. The already selective information supply has narrowed down even more and occupies the user's reality to a certain extent. For example, if a platform almost exclusively recommends content around certain political views, it's likely to significantly color the user's reality. This individual may share his reality with the echo chamber but he's likely to be alienated from what's outside of it.

Also, social scientists have defined a phenomenon called 'motivational reasoning.' People often aren't rational and objective in their reasoning, and often already have specific conclusions in mind, and simply use their reasoning as a way to support their claims. Motivational reasoning, therefore, is biased. Echo chambers most likely enforce our bias.

Suppose, for example, a group of Dutch people in an echo chamber strongly believe that all Belgians are stupid. Within the echo chamber, this notion that Belgians are stupid gets repeated so many times that its members accept it as a truth. These Dutch people are so obsessed with their southern neighbors' alleged stupidity that they're continually looking for any news or rumors about it. Now, as soon a Belgian indeed does something slightly unintelligent (and this hits the news for some reason), they immediately pick it up and say: "See? Again, we have proof that *all* Belgians are stupid."

Things change but actually don't

Although time seems to pass by linearly, it also moves in cyclical patterns. We move forward in time, but we're also on repeat. The passage of time is like a song played over and over again, perhaps with a few variations, and changes of instruments, but it's essentially the same. Marcus Aurelius beautifully described the continual repetition of things and that, in essence, nothing new happens. Everything is familiar and transient. He asked: "Which is why observing life for forty years is as good as a thousand. Would you really see anything new?"

One empire succeeds the other, and after thousands of years, this pattern hasn't changed. We can

170

say the same about violence, sports competitions, politics, and hostility between cultures and nations. History repeats itself, sometimes day after day, sometimes millennium after millennium. So, we could ask ourselves how important the news actually is if they essentially bring nothing new. Isn't all the tragedy we see in the media just a dramatization of the same old worldly winds that have been blowing since the dawn of time?

Henry David Thoreau was critical of the value of the majority of communications. He mentioned, for example, that he never received more than one or two letters worth the postage. About the news, which he saw as the equivalent of gossip, he wrote the following:

> " (...) I am sure that I never read any memorable news in a newspaper. If we read of one man robbed, or murdered, or killed by accident, or one house burned, or one vessel wrecked, or one steamboat blown up, or one cow run over on the Western Railroad, or one mad dog killed, or one lot of grasshoppers in the winter,—we never need read of another. One is enough. If you are acquainted with the principle, what do you care for a myriad of instances and applications?"

Henry David Thoreau, *Walden*, Where I Lived, and What I Lived For

To the things that repeat themselves, we can also add the phenomenon of rumors about possible threats. How many times should WWIII have broken out already? Sure, this possibility is present, and it probably will happen someday. It might even have already happened when you're reading this. But things happen when they happen, and living in constant fear and speculation doesn't change it. When we look at these rumors from a distance, we'll see the principle of *fear-mongering* behind it, serving as a way to attract attention and make bank. And that it's just another pattern that has been going on for ages.

We create the world

Is the world as terrible as we think? It depends on how we see it. There's a difference between how we see things and how they truly are. Because of the limitations of our senses and comprehension, we'll never see how things exactly are. But within the bandwidth of our limited perceptions, we can still differentiate between clarity and delusion. A clear vision of the world aligns with reality, at least as much as possible. Someone with a clear vision doesn't necessarily deny the validity of the information stream, but remains skeptical, puts it in perspective, and knows that the vast majority of the circulating information isn't a big deal. The input of disturbing news is not proportionate to what's going on at large. It's just a tiny pixel in the vastness of reality, selected, magnified, and presented engagingly.

In a way, today's many forms of news present themselves as a giant soap opera. But instead of using *fictional* characters and stories, they use fragments of reality and dramatize them for entertainment value. All fun and games, but it's not a good representation of reality.

The world, as a whole, is a pretty dull place. For every person murdered, billions aren't. For every volcano eruption, there are hundreds of millions of square kilometers of tranquil land. Ages pass, repeating the same things in different packaging. Today's hottest topic is tomorrow's old news, and most of it is soon to be forgotten. And even though today's catastrophes replace yesterday's drama, it's nothing compared to the overall tranquility we'll find when we turn *off* our televisions, computers, and smartphones and just go for a walk outside. Even in most cities, we'll discover that things are just going on as they do: people walking their dogs, cars passing by, a homeless person sleeping on a bench. Also, in times of turmoil that temporarily dysregulate human life, trees continue to grow calmy, and so do birds and flowers that appear in spring and the Sun in the East every morning.

Suppose we keep reminding ourselves of today's mass information supply's delusional nature and experience reality without distortion. In that case, we'll see that the real world presents us with significantly less tragedy compared to the screen. Whether Earth is beautiful or not is ultimately in the eye of the beholder. But if we lose touch with reality, by diving into that seductive, carefully selected puddle of doom and gloom, then mud is all we'll see. And what could be beautiful eludes us.

Falling Into Place

Based on stories told by Buddhist monk Ajahn Brahm

A man is chased by a tiger. Suddenly, he encounters an abandoned well. He jumps in, hoping that the tiger can't reach him there. But then he realizes that there's a venomous snake at the bottom of this dried-out well. Before he reaches the bottom, he grabs a root poking out of the wall and holds on. The tiger looks at him from the top, waiting for him to get out, and the snake is waiting at the bottom for him to fall down. Shortly after, two mice appear from a hole in the wall and start chewing on the root he's holding on to.

Now, what to do next?

It's no secret that life can be very difficult and painful. And sometimes we're running from our problems only to run into more difficulties. When our sense of security is stripped away from us, we come to realize that we are at the mercy of an uncontrollable and terrible fate: everything is falling apart, there seems to be nothing we can do about it and we've got no place to run. When we're hanging onto a root that's chewed away by mice with a hungry snake below and an even hungrier tiger above us, what can we possibly do to get out of this situation? What is the best course of action when there seems to be no way out? When life seems to be falling apart, is it actually falling into place?

An act of rebellion

It's not the circumstances that make us miserable, but how we *perceive* these circumstances. Even though the man hanging between a tiger and a snake is powerless when it comes to his external circumstances; it's his perception that decides his mood. Knowing that this is a Buddhist story, it's probably no surprise that this man has been practicing at his local temple, and is pretty aware of what the Buddha called the 'eight worldly winds', which are pleasure and pain, gain and loss, praise and blame, fame and disrepute.

Most people are controlled by the eight worldly winds. When they're in pain, they suffer. When they experience pleasure, they're joyful. When their reputation goes down the drain, they become depressed. But when they're famous and loved, they're ecstatic. The problem with this way of life is the slavish relationship with the environment that goes with it, as external things decide our mood, while these same external things are not up to us. So, when our happiness depends on the behavior of the eight worldly winds, we're in a very unreliable position.

Without a doubt, the average person would probably be frightened when hanging between a snake and a tiger, waiting for the only sense of security to be eaten away by mice. But as an avid practitioner of Buddhism, this man isn't afraid at all, and calmly observes the situation. Then, he suddenly sees honey that is dripping from a beehive sitting in a tree above the well. He smiles and starts licking the honey. In the face of misery, finding such joy can be considered mutiny against the system. Because even when the most terrible circumstances won't stop him from enjoying what the present moment has to offer, he has claimed *true freedom* from the fickleness of a universe that enslaves most of its subjects; the poor souls whose lives are nothing but the suffering of its whims.

The man in the well knew that he shouldn't panic or burst out in anger, as the situation he's in is to be expected: the occurrence of unpleasant or even life-threatening events is an unavoidable part of life. So, the best thing he could do is to find joy in his darkest hour; something that, as opposed to his predicament, lies within his field of control. But there was something else that made him decide to stay calm and collected while hanging between the tiger and the snake. During his Buddhist practice, he learned the truth about existence, which he reminded himself of when life goes well, and also when life falls apart.

The future may surprise you

That change occurs is certain. We just don't know where change will bring us. But when we're finding ourselves in dire straits, and there seems no way out, it's essential to always remember that everything changes. The worldly winds are unpredictable. One moment they provide us with delight, the other moment with agony.

Once upon a time, there was an Eastern king who was overjoyed and overconfident when times were good, but depressed when times were bad. So, the sage handed him a ring with a simple sentence engraved in it: "This too shall pass". The ring reminded him every day of the transient nature of life. When times were good, he prepared for bad times, and when times were bad, he was certain that how permanent and unescapable these moments seemed: they too shall pass.

However, the power of change is often underestimated because we're unable to foresee the future. When we're stuck in our perception of the current situation, it's difficult to conceive how the future may play out, as there are so many variables and so many possibilities. People in despair commonly believe that their misery is never-ending, as the light at the end of the tunnel has yet to present itself. They're stuck in a mere perception of what's happening at a particular moment, without taking into consideration that change is occurring in the background.

The 'reality' we base our assessments on is shifting. Thus, what we perceive as our life falling apart, may actually be our life falling into place oftentimes in ways that we don't expect. We do know by experience that, in most cases, the future plays out differently than we had previously expected. Moreover, it's not unlikely that the future unfolds in ways that are nothing less than surprising. Surprise overcame the man in the well, whose fate seemed to be sealed, but was flabbergasted when the tiger, hungry as it was, leaned too much to the front, fell into the well right past the man, squashed the snake, and broke his neck by the fall. And so, the man was able to climb out and survive.

No matter how miserable things seem at the moment, the solution may be at our doorstep, as the course of the wind changes to our advantage. So, again, when life seems to fall apart, it may actually be falling into place.

But regardless of how things play out, we'll never know beforehand what Fortune will bring us. This means that it's futile to hope for a certain outcome. As the Stoic philosopher, Epictetus put it: "Don't demand that things happen as you wish, but wish that they happen as they do happen, and you will go on well." Sometimes there's just nothing we can do about the circumstances we're in, no matter how painful, which was the case with the man in the well. But we *can* choose the position we take towards these circumstances. Pain is certain. Suffering is optional. So, do we give unpleasant circumstances the power to make us miserable, or do we enjoy some honey instead?

Problems

Two people attend a house party, where they socialize with the same guests, drink from the same beer tap, and are exposed to the same music and atmosphere. They decide to share a taxi and drive home when the party is over as they live closely together. "That party really sucked," one person says. "The beer was terrible, the DJ was awful, and the guests were insufferable." Then the other person says smiling joyfully: "Really? I just had the best party in years."

The above shows how different we see, in essence, the same thing. How come someone experiences outside events as very pleasurable while another person is annoyed by the same circumstances? It seems that everyone has different interpretations of what's happening around them. What's gold for someone is mud to someone else. So, what's preferable, unpleasant, beautiful, or undesirable, although consensus exists, ultimately lies in the eye of the beholder.

Nevertheless, many people have difficulties seeing their realities for what they are: *subjective*, based on opinion, and not the absolute truth. If someone believes a party inherently sucks, then this person doesn't see it as a mere observation but as a fact. And as a consequence, the person believes he suffers from the party, but in reality, he suffers from his attitude towards it.

The party itself cannot cause suffering. Just like we can't listen to music without ears or taste food without a tongue, something can only be suffered if there's a sufferer. The party needs something to observe and interpret. And thus, in reality, problems cannot exist without a perceiver, as circumstances aren't troublesome without someone or something *identifying* them as such. So, if there's nothing inherently problematic about reality, doesn't that mean that we humans repeatedly (and on a grand scale) worry about problems that don't even exist?

The many different worlds

Before we try to answer whether or not our problems actually exist, we'll explore the nature of reality in the light of Eastern philosophical ideas. After all, most (if not all) issues relate to our circumstances; to what we perceive as reality. For example, according to our collectively agreed-upon norms, 'having financial problems' means that we cannot pay off debts over the long or short term or pay for our living expenses. And since we cannot meet the norms, we consider our situation 'problematic.'

But regardless of the discomfort that financial problems bring, the problematic element we attach to it remains *subjective*. It's a consequence of a collective *perception* of reality, labeling appearances right or wrong, valuable or not valuable, desirable or undesirable.

As human beings, reality as we experience it consists of countless concepts and ideas. These help us make sense of chaos by naming things, using labels, bundling elements together, distinguishing one thing from the other, and applying value judgments. These concepts and ideas can be collective and individual, meaning that the human world consists of billions of 'sub-worlds' which are all realities on their own. Hence, in one person's universe, a party is fantastic. In another, it's lame.

Also, human reality isn't the only reality out there. Animals, and possibly even plants, have their unique perceptions of reality. The world of dogs primarily consists of smells, for example. Dogs cannot reason like humans and don't understand concepts like 'capitalism,' or 'religion,' or 'financial problems.' And because they cannot comprehend these concepts, they won't cause them any concern. Dogs are concerned with food, protecting their loved ones, and bodily affection, which are traits we share. And so, the worlds of humans and dogs intersect but are still very different from each other.

The Taoist scripture *Zhuangzi* mentions a parable about the human concept of beauty. In the story, two women considered most attractive by men were rather repulsive in the eyes of other living creatures:

"Mao Qiang and Li Ji were accounted by men to be most beautiful, but when fishes saw them, they dived deep in the water from them; when birds,

they flew from them aloft; and when deer saw them, they separated and fled away."

Zhuangzi, Inner Chapters, The Adjustment of Controversies, par. 11

Could it be that the fish, birds, and deer simply have bad taste? Or could it be that our value judgments, even if the whole of humanity agrees upon them, aren't universally true?

Looking from Zhuangzi's perspective, the most reasonable answer is that human perception of beauty is not universal, nor is the perception of animals. Attractive beauty in a dog's eyes is probably another dog, in the eyes of a snake, another snake, in the eyes of a human being, another human being. But none of these creatures has a monopoly on beauty itself. Therefore, beauty is not universal but created by the perceiver.

No matter if we look at the world as humans or fish, our realities are subjective, restricted to our unique worlds of experience. So, human problems aren't generally dog problems. And what seem problems to one person often aren't problems to another.

Two truths

In Buddhism, there's a concept called the 'two truths,' which distinguishes between relative truth (or conventional truth) and absolute truth (the world as it is). The concept is much debated, and there isn't a consensus on the absolute truth, probably because it's pretty difficult to conceptualize what we cannot cognitively experience.

Some argue that the absolute truth is emptiness, and if we manage to look past the illusion, we can experience that, in reality, nothing is there. And so, the actual universe goes beyond the senses. The Taoists call this absolute truth 'Tao,' and Lao Tzu described it as follows:

The Tao is like an empty container:
it can never be emptied and can never be filled.
Infinitely deep, it is the source of all things.
It dulls the sharp, unties the knotted,
shades the lighted, and unites all of creation with dust.

It is hidden but always present.
I don't know who gave birth to it.
It is older than the concept of God.

Lao Tzu, *Tao Te Ching*, 4

But we *could* say, with relative certainty, that the concept signifies how we perceive the universe differs from the actual universe itself. Our senses determine our perception of the universe; we can only witness the world as far as our senses allow us to. And from this limited perception arises our relative truth, as is the case with dogs, fishes, and deer.

Relative truth is subjective. The notion that a party 'sucks' isn't less valid than the opinion that the party is 'fantastic.' Isn't the same true regarding our problems? What's problematic to one isn't problematic to another. Problems, therefore, are also subjective. They're among the layer of conventional truth that obscures the absolute truth; they are as illusory as everything else our minds create. They are a perception of reality, not reality itself. They're mere interpretations of the circumstances, not the circumstances. They don't exist in the 'absolute reality' because if they did, everyone else would have encountered them as well. So, outside of our perceptions, there is no problem. In the same way, there is no dog; at least not our human concept of it.

Yet, problems appear very real to those who manufacture them. We tend to suffer them endlessly, so the pain they cause is heartfelt. And, unfortunately, we're masters at creating these problems as well.

The problem machine

An investor notices that his stocks have lost twenty percent of their value in a single day. He panics and can barely keep it together. But another investor who experiences the same twenty percent decline is delighted, as she now has an opportunity to purchase stocks at a bargain. Again, because of our subjective realities, whether something appears problematic differs per person. On top of that, we see that solving *one* problem often leads to *another* problem. Some people just dwell in a perpetual stream of "issues" regardless of how many of them they solve.

For example, a week later, the twenty percent drop has changed to a thirty percent increase, which means the previous problem (the twenty percent drop) has been solved. But the first investor then starts worrying that he didn't buy the dip, and thus he missed out on potential profit. He's even more distressed when he discovers that the other investor did buy the dip. So, even though his portfolio increased by ten percent, he still perceives his situation as problematic.

And so, it's with many things in life. There's always *someone* creating problems out of situations that aren't necessarily bad. And then, if the problems get solved, this person examines the status quo to propose even more problems. People with such fault-finding mindsets can endlessly solve issues by altering circumstances; it's just a matter of time until new ones arise. No set of circumstances will end their problems if they keep creating them.

Solving versus dissolving

There's a consensus among many that we should deal with problems by solving them. Therefore, problems become nails to be hammered. And if they aren't hammered, they'll be sticking out of the wall forever. There certainly are situations that pose a direct threat to our safety (or other people's safety) that require action. And some tend to be sticky and very difficult to tolerate, and thus we're probably better off *doing* something about them.

However, our problems don't need to be solved in many cases. After all, they are creations of a fault-finding mind and don't represent reality in itself. *Anything* can be considered problematic. Take, for example, a situation in which people dislike your physical appearance. Why does this appear as a problem? Because you're worried about other people's opinions. So, there are two things you can do: the first one is to try and (quote-unquote) "solve" your problem by changing your appearance, perhaps dressing differently, getting a haircut or lip fillers, as an attempt for people to like you.

The second one is to *let go* of the problem altogether, which, in this case, means that you accept your appearance and let go of the desire to be liked by those people. After all, the people disliking you aren't a problem in itself; the mind makes it so. But a dog couldn't care less what people think of his appearance and doesn't care about yours either. So, being unattractive in the eyes of others may be an everyday human problem; it's definitely not absolute. So, is it really a problem then? The problem vanishes by embracing the circumstances as they are and not wishing to change anything about them. So, instead of *solving* them by rearranging the environment, we can *dissolve* them by letting them go. In essence, it's what *meditation* does, as it decreases the discursive thinking patterns generating these problems in the first place. Buddhist scholar Gil Fronsdal stated the following:

> *"Rather than directly solving our personal problems, non-action and meditation can help us to step away from our preoccupation with our problems, and this change in emphasis can sometimes make space for new solutions to arise or for the problem itself to diminish on its own. Some problems are better dissolved than solved."*

Gil Fronsdal, *The Action of Non-Action*

Often, when we solve a problem, we essentially *change* our circumstances in our favor. But the caveat is that our circumstances are out of control, meaning that if we experience our circumstances as problematic, we find fault in something in which we ultimately have no say. After solving a specific problem, it can appear again after circumstances change. Problem-solving, therefore, isn't always efficient, as the ever-changing universe can easily undo our efforts. Changing the *experience* of our circumstances lies *within* our control.

Changing our *attitude* is much more efficient and realistic than changing the *world*. Instead of changing outside occurrences to solve what we recognize as 'problems,' we could also *free* ourselves from these problems by letting the discursive activities in our minds dissolve. Here's where the illusory nature of our problems works to our advantage: problems don't exist outside our perception. At the same time, our thoughts are very inconsistent, and our attitude towards the environment changes, often without us even realizing it. We can painfully worry about a situation but have entirely *lost* these worries later. How come something that so heavily occupied us a few days ago seems relatively insignificant today? Have the circumstances changed? Or have *we* changed?

Many people experience an altered mindset when they're drunk or under the influence of certain substances. Their day-to-day worries often disappear, and the world seems radically different and much less gloomy. But no radical changes took place in the world. What's drastically changed, however, are their mental states. Although temporarily effective, narcotics may not be the healthiest way to dissolve one's problems. Moreover, people often see their problems and worries reappear after the "high" subsides, sometimes even louder and more robust. There are healthier ways to dissolve our problems, for example, by contemplating the nature of reality and the vastness of the universe. Or we could shift our focus from the situation to its silver lining.

Buddhists get to the root of the issue through meditation by calming the great manufacturer of all things horrible, also known as the mind. When the mind settles down, problems disappear, and all we're left with are the intrinsically *neutral* outside circumstances. And so, eventually, the world gets pretty OK as it is, and the problems we *thought* we had, don't seem problems at all.

Radical Acceptance

Some experiences weigh on us like a heavy cross that's almost impossible to bear. They paralyze us with guilt or make us hide in shame. And in other cases, they leave us with an immense amount of pain for us to process. Many people either fight or stick their heads in the sand, and never come to terms with how things are. But there's a way to move forward. And it starts with accepting reality for what it is, which, in some cases, is an act of radicalism.

Imagine that someone sticks you with a knife. There are several things you can do. You can ignore it. Or you can try to fight it, and resist the fact that it happened. But the only thing that eventually leads to healing, is the acceptance that this event – regardless of its brutality – took place. I know this is kind of a harsh example, but moving forward in any situation, and also finding ways to truly process it, is done by acceptance. Now, this doesn't mean that we condone or approve of anything. It means that we honestly *acknowledge* what's going on in our environment and in ourselves.

Many people often look at *acceptance* as a form of *giving in*. They see it as a weakness. But is there anything weaker than refusing to observe things how they really are? And to purposefully live in a state of blissful ignorance, simply because we don't want to be confronted with the harsh reality? It's no surprise that human beings often engage in the most creative ways of sugarcoating, downplaying, ignoring, and denying. We push trauma into the shadows of our psyche, we drink away our pain, or even create a complete web of lies that protect us from realizing what's truly going on. These are just coping mechanisms in order to stay away from the ugliness of truth.

People get stuck for many years – in some cases for a lifetime – because they refuse to confront what they've been running from. A lifetime of denial can eat someone from the inside out. It creates cognitive dissonance; from silently sticking one's head in the sand, to violently lashing out as a defense mechanism. When we find ourselves in a position of pain, no matter how horrendous it is, the only way to get unstuck is acceptance. And when the pain is overwhelming, and the reality seems too heavy to bear, then, the act of acceptance becomes *radical*. Especially when we've been lying to ourselves for such a long time, and our minds have become pressure cookers that are about to explode. And also, when the things we accept, are in conflict with our ideas and beliefs about how life ought to be.

Radical acceptance means that we acknowledge the stuff that's excruciatingly painful. When we accept, we let go and when we let go, we stop worrying. Things like parental abuse, characteristics about ourselves that we hate, the fact that we're suffering an illness (perhaps a lethal one), or crimes we've committed in the past, and the guilt that comes from that. But it's necessary to finally let go, and get past the things we've been resisting for so long. Because what we resist, persists. And what we accept, we move beyond. Some things are up to us, some things aren't. We can't change the past. We have no certainties about the future. However, we *do* control the position we take toward life. As Søren Kierkegaard stated: *"Life can only be understood backward, but it must be lived forwards."*

So, what are we going to do? Are we going to hide from the truth? Or fight reality? Live in the past? Or will we muster the courage to accept the present and everything in it, so we can move forward, and mold the ugliness of this moment into a better future? We cannot change things for the better when we don't acknowledge them. We won't put a bandage on a wound if we *deny* its existence in the first place. And if we live life ignorantly, based on lies, we might try to change a *false reality*, which is kind of insane, and also counterproductive.

Radical acceptance is a powerful act. It means that we take a deep breath, stand up straight, with our shoulders back, and look the abyss straight in the eye. It sends a message to the outside world that we are willing to embrace it, that we don't cower away from the consequences of doing so, and that we're confident that we'll find a way to deal with it.